# School of Tomorrow

*A Study of a Comprehensive School in a
North West Newtown*

JOHN MAYS

WILLIAM QUINE

KATHLEEN PICKETT

A report of a research project carried out by members of the
Department of Social Science in the University of Liverpool

LONGMAN

LONGMAN GROUP LIMITED
*Associated companies, branches and representatives*
*throughout the world*

© *Longman Group Ltd ( formerly Longmans, Green & Co Ltd ) 1968*
All rights reserved. No part of this publication may be
reproduced, stored in a retrieval system, or transmitted in any
form or by any means, electronic, mechanical, photocopying,
recording, or otherwise, without the prior permission of the
Copyright owner.

*First published 1968*
*Second impression 1970*

SBN 582 32050 X

Printed in Great Britain by
Lowe & Brydone (Printers) Ltd., London

# Contents

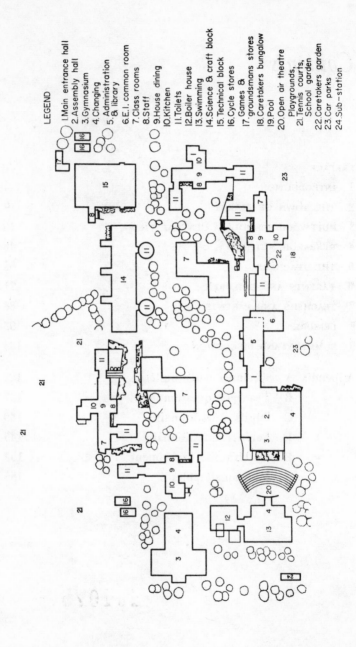

LEGEND

1. Main entrance hall
2. Assembly hall
3. Gymnasium
4. Changing
5. Administration
6. E.I. common room
7. Class rooms
8. library
9. Staff
10. House dining
11. Kitchen
12. Toilets
13. Boiler house
14. Swimming
15. Science & craft block
16. Technical block
17. Cycle stores
18. Games
19. groundsmans stores
20. Caretakers bungalow
21. Pool
22. Open air theatre
Playgrounds,
21. Tennis courts,
School garden
22. Caretakers garden
23. Car parks
24. Sub-station

# *Preface*

In presenting this short research report to a wider public there
are two points I would like to make on behalf of the colleagues
in the Department who shared the tasks of acquiring the data
and writing this account with me. In the first place, we are
very conscious of the inadequacy of what we have done and
were it not for the fact that so few case studies of English
schools exist we would not have been so presumptious as to
proceed to publication. Secondly, I would like to thank all
those who participated in the research and helped us either by
supplying information or being patient enough to answer our
questions. To the parents we visited in their homes, to the
pupils we questioned at school and to the staff who responded
to our questionnaire and gave us personal advice and encouragement we would like to say a very warm and sincere thank
you. We are also grateful to Mr Percy Lord, the county Chief
Education Officer, and to the Governors of the school both for
official permission to undertake the enquiry and for authority
to publish our results and comments. Finally, and above all,
we must express our deep indebtedness to the headmaster, Mr
Allan Barnes, for his help and support for without him, in a
very literal sense, this research would never have been undertaken. It was, in fact, originally at his invitation that I first
visited the school and initiated the project. We apologise to
all who co-operated for the shortcomings of this survey. Its
faults and blemishes are entirely our responsibility. We trust,
however, that in spite of these some teachers and organisers
will find points of interest in our report and if in some small
way we have contributed anything to the cause of educational
advance this will be justification enough. Be that as it may,
I conclude by wishing even greater success to the school itself
in the long years of work which lie before it.

JOHN MAYS.

University of Liverpool,
Department of Social Science.
*October* 1967.

*Disce Vivere* (Learn how to Live). These words, taken by Ruffwood School as its motto, are part of an inscription on the cross in Kirkby churchyard marking the site of the altar of the original Saxon church.

# I

# *Introduction*

## *I*

This book is a study of one particular comprehensive school operating in a new housing area in the North West of England. In the chapters that follow we will endeavour to describe this school in as much detail and as accurately as possible, drawing to a considerable extent on answers to questions which research workers put to samples of pupils and parents at a particular point of time, and on the responses of all those members of the teaching staff who agreed to collaborate with the investigators. At a later stage we will outline the actual research procedures followed, but before doing so it is necessary to give a general description of the school itself and of the area in which it is located. These introductory descriptive chapters will, we hope, enable the reader to see the school as an institution functioning in a specific physical and social environment. We think they will also enable the reader to see something of the organisational problems which confront such a school without overlooking the personal and human aspects of the educational process. It is a constant danger of sociological analysis that it inevitably tends towards abstractions, impersonal assessments and generalisation. But education is primarily about people: their feelings, attitudes, motivations. In a research report of this nature it is tremendously difficult to convey this essentially human aspect of the educational process as it operates in a particular institution. Wherever possible we have interpolated into the text comments made to us by various individuals, partly to illustrate a general point but partly also to try to convey a little of the 'feel' of the real life situation which we were privileged to study.

The enquiry was carried out by members of the staff of the Department of Social Science in the University of Liverpool. It is to be evaluated as part of an ongoing research effort which began in the mid nineteen-fifties when the community research team undertook a survey of the social background and family life of a central residential area in the Victorian heart of the City of Liverpool.[1] It so happened that a substantial proportion of families who had lived in this 'down town' locality were moved by the Corporation to the new housing area of Kirkby in South Lancashire, some seven miles distant from the city centre. In 1960 the Department undertook a follow-up study of some of these families and of similar families rehoused from Liverpool. An initial account of this research has already been published in the *Sociological Review*[2] and the material collected by the field workers then will be used to supplement other basic data throughout this report and more especially in Chapter Two.

Part of the original Crown Street enquiry was directed at an analysis of the educational provision in the survey area and this was printed separately in a volume entitled *Education and the Urban Child*.[3] The conclusions reached in this latter book were of such a nature that it was natural that we should, when time and opportunity became available, try to follow up the scholastic experiences of these ex-citydweller's children in the new school buildings in the new areas and see whether any marked change had occurred. The main findings of *Education and the Urban Child* were that, for a variety of reasons—including inadequate parental support, inferior school buildings and equipment, deficiencies amongst the teaching staffs themselves and a generally apathetic attitude to academic work all round—the children of the 'down town' schools were seriously underrated and gravely underprivileged. These findings were, a short time later, massively vindicated

[1] C. Vereker, J. B. Mays, E. Gittus and M. Broady *Urban Redevelopment and Social Change*, Liverpool University Press, 1961.
[2] See N. H. Rankin 'Social Adjustment in a North West Newtown' *Sociological Review*, vol. II, No. 3, November 1963, pp. 289-302.
[3] J. B. Mays, Liverpool University Press, 2nd impression, 1965.

for similarly placed schools throughout the whole country by the publication of the now famous Newsom Committee's report, *Half Our Future*,[1] which revealed that no less than two-fifths of all the so-called modern schools were at that time 'seriously deficient in many respects'. The schools in the old slum neighbourhoods were, as might be expected, the least satisfactory of all. Since a great many of the Kirkby families had come from neighbourhoods served by these Newsom type schools, it seemed clear that what was taking place in the new residential area involved a social experiment of quite unusually vital significance. It is not often that social scientists have a chance to study the process of social change at something like first hand and so, when our departmental research interests swung towards Kirkby, we looked around for an opportunity to extend our enquiries into the scholastic field. Unfortunately, it was not possible with the slender resources at our disposal to do more than take one bite at the cherry and we had perforce to be content with a detailed study of only one of the four secondary schools which serve the new estate. The school we elected for the research cannot be regarded as typical of all Kirkby schools, although no doubt many of the problems which we encountered there will be found at the three others. It must be made clear at the outset, however, that we are not offering this report as a description of a typical Kirkby secondary school, let alone of a typical comprehensive school. We believe that the study will be of interest to educationalists in its own right, as a case study of a large school. We further believe that at a time when comprehensive education is the avowed ultimate educational goal of the present national government, there is a crying need for as much factual information about the working of such schools as can be collected. It is only by the compilation of similar case studies, their careful analysis and comparison with other forms of secondary schooling, that an objective, rational and informed public opinion on so hotly debated a public issue can possibly be formed. We think that these two reasons are ample justification, if such be needed, for the publication of this book.

[1] H.M.S.O., 1963.

## II

Educational sociologists may find this account of a new kind of school in a new area of particular interest in view of the general debate which takes place amongst sociological theorists regarding the appropriate model to be utilised in explaining the nature of social relationships in an industrial community. Very crudely, the two extreme models most frequently offered us are those which see social relationships predominantly characterised on the one hand by conflict, on the other by consensus.[1] These two explanations are sometimes presented as dichotomous alternatives; we select either one or the other. The conflict model is derived ultimately from the general Marxist notion of the class war and involves underprivileged classes wresting their educational rights from a controlling powerful elite group which wishes to offer them only so much literacy as may enable them to be more richly exploited in the economic and commercial sense by their masters. In the light of this kind of analysis the working class majority must obtain education in order to fight and eventually overcome the bourgeoisie for the control of the community. The W.E.A. and the Adult Education movements of the not too distant past epitomise this kind of approach which at a much more militant level was conspicuous in the activities of the Plebs League and in the founding of the extreme left-wing communist-syndicalist London College, by a breakaway group from more gradualist policies in 1910.[2] Both the militant Left and the reformist Left saw education primarily as an arena of conflict between the two major classes and believed that by the achievement of more knowledge the workers would be enabled to change the existing social stratification of the country. There was no real attempt to take over the existing traditional academic institutions—the grammar and public schools and the universities. Rather the effort lay in the direction of founding alternative educational organisations in which the members of the working

[1] For a recent British discussion of this see John Rex *Key Problems of Sociological Theory*, Routledge and Kegan Paul, 1961.
[2] *The Times*, 16 April 1912, p. 7.

class would be helped to equip themselves for ultimate social victory. The London School of Economics was founded very much in this tradition.

The contrary model based on the idea of consensus may be traced in the pioneering educational sociology of Durkheim, who very briefly, thought of education as a powerful social-ising agency whose purpose it was to provide fundamental cohesion to the entire society. The task of the teacher was, in this view, mainly to pass on the traditional cultural values while the school operated as an instrument of social control. Moral imperatives hence formed a fundamental part of the teacher's role as Durkheim saw it, for 'as the priest is the interpreter of his god, the teacher is the interpreter of the great moral ideas of his times and of his country.'[1] Although Durkheim was not oblivious of the need for social change or of the contribution that education should make to this end. his attitude does seem to have been mainly influenced by a strong desire to achieve consensus. Even the 'ultimate object of every pedagogical reform' was, to use his own expression, to try to make students 'more men of their time'.

It is probably true to say that until comparatively recent years the generally accepted function of education has been to preserve the existing social and moral order and to safeguard the rising generation against corrupting influences. A careful examination of the history of English education published in the mid nineteen-fifties concluded that, in regard to its influence as an agent of social change, 'the system of secondary education had played a relatively passive role'.[2] The conclusion was reached that the social system influenced educational institutions rather than the other way round. Bright and ambitious lower class pupils could make their way up the social ladder by means of the scholarship system, but social mobility fostered in this way did as much to reinforce the existing social system as to modify its dominance or change

[1] E. Durkheim *Education and Sociology*, translated with an introduction by Sherwood D. Fox, foreword by Talcott Parsons. The Free Press, 1958, p. 89.
[2] O. Banks, *Parity and Prestige in English Secondary Education*, Routledge & Kegan Paul, 1955, p. 248.

its objectives. But, since the 1944 Education Act, there have been signs that the educational system can be, and indeed has been, used as a vehicle for social change which in some respects is revolutionary in its potentialities if not yet markedly in its results. It is not merely that opportunities have become more equal, that more and more children from working class family backgrounds have been academically ushered into and welcomed by the meritocracy.[1] Something much more significant has happened with the development of comprehensive schools. Here we have what in this country is an altogether novel situation in which both the model based on consensus and that based on conflict are to some extent relevant yet not entirely adequate. Comprehensive schools are the latter-day descendants of the older socialist-inspired educational institutions which aimed, if not at the social dominance of any one class, at least at the overthrow of superior group status and the elimination of traditional inequalities. If we may anticipate the main body of our report for a moment to quote the words of one of those who answered our questions: the comprehensive school 'has one purpose (among many) which is distinctive. It aims consciously (or at any rate should) at *a classless society*'.

Such a comment as the above implies not so much a conflict as a socially creative function for education. What elements of conflict still exist are certainly not the old and simple divisions between the 'haves' and the 'have nots'. They are much more clearly to be understood in terms of a conflict of cultural values. Teachers in a comprehensive secondary school serving a mainly one class locality such as we have studied by and large represent the values which the more thoughtful and liberal minded members of the successful middle class espouse and seek to propagate. It is not, as we shall try to show in more detail later, that the school stands crudely for the bourgeois values and way of life over and against the traditional working class pattern. The situation in such a community is much more complex and subtle. The comprehensive school may

[1] For example, the increased proportion of students from working class backgrounds who now read for a university degree today compared with, say, thirty years ago.

have a social mission. It can be an instrument of reform. But part of its mission seems to involve persuading working class people to adopt some of the behaviour forms associated in the past with 'superior' social groups, while, at the same time, reinforcing the traditional strengths of established working class communities. The socialisation process to which the pupils are exposed is not designed, as it is in the case of private and public schools and direct grant and older grammar schools also to a considerable extent, to confirm the code of values which teachers and parents have in common. It is rather to persuade both pupils and parents to adopt new attitudes and to accept standards which are partially alien to them and, perhaps in some instances, positively inimical. It seeks to do this, moreover, for ideological and moral reasons rather than simply to increase the nation's economic efficiency, although the latter is not to be thought of as an unimportant result of the provision of a genuine secondary education to groups which have hitherto been denied this opportunity.

Such a view of education as the active agent promoting social change is undoubtedly a new one in British society. When universal elementary schooling was provided after the 1870 Act it was not seen as a step in the direction of greater social equality so much as a recognition of the fact that industry required a better equipped force of manual labour. The Butler Act of 1944, which affirmed the principle that every child in the country, irrespective of family background, should *as a matter of right* receive that kind of education for which his abilities suited him, showed the way to a future social order for which the concept of the common school is the logical corollary.

Our study of one large comprehensive school is an attempt to illustrate its work in terms of the above analysis. We will look at it in the guise of a vehicle of social change and see how, in the light of this new social function, the task of the teacher is also modified in terms of the needs of the neighbourhood it serves. It would be a mistake, however, to suggest that the comprehensive school, wherever it is to be found, is always to be thought of in identical terms. Comprehensive schools have been established in vastly dissimilar parts of the country in the years following the Second World War and, while in the London area they have had a specific socio-political objective, in predominantly rural areas, such as Anglesey in North Wales, the decision to establish such a system was, to a great extent, influenced by rational economic and administrative considerations. There is, hence, no such thing as 'a comprehensive school movement' which is utterly committed to a particular political philosophy and, in truly British fashion, a variety of experiments have been made in different parts of the country in an attempt to meet local needs and pressures. Amongst these, the Leicestershire Plan, which tries to amalgamate existing grammar schools with modern schools in a new comprehensive structure, is perhaps the most widely known.

Nevertheless, in the area in which this research was carried out it seems clear to us that the particular school we studied is dedicated to the promotion of social change and that, in such a situation, the role of the teacher is modified in important and possibly novel ways. We can perhaps best suggest this by saying that to the traditional aspects of the teacher's role as purveyor of knowledge, moral mentor and cultural missionary there has been added the further task of acting as agent of social reform.

# 2

# *The Town of Kirkby*

## *I*

Kirkby, on the monotonously flat, wet plain of South-West Lancashire, is separated by only a short green belt from its giant neighbour, the city and seaport of Liverpool. As a new development it falls under none of the three usually applicable headings: housing estate, expanded town and New Town. It is, in fact, an expanded housing estate, for the original Kirkby settlement was of only 3,000 men and women, mainly concerned with agriculture. The new houses and flats were built by Liverpool for Liverpool families, but on land within the jurisdiction of Lancashire County Council, who provided 'county' services. Although the County has been under great pressure from Liverpool to transfer the area to the City, this has never been done, and in 1958 Kirkby became an Urban District. Its population in 1965 was estimated at 60,000.

The area was chosen for large scale housing development because a trading estate owned by Liverpool Corporation, about a mile away, was already in existence. This had been built on the site of a large Royal Ordnance factory constructed during the war and bought by Liverpool in 1947. The trading estate was successfully developed, and particularly rapid expansion took place after Merseyside's designation as a Development Area in 1949, when it qualified for favoured treatment by the Board of Trade in its distribution of Industrial Development Certificates. Main services, some new roads and public transport, and potential employment opportunities were therefore already in the vicinity of Kirkby and these factors together with a large area of land available for housing appeared to make it an ideal situation for a new community.

The original plan, drawn up by Lancashire County Council as the statutory planning authority, was for 40,000 people, to be housed in fifteen years. This was modified under Liverpool's urgent representations to 50,000 people within six years. Even before the war, Liverpool had a serious housing problem and an ambitious programme of slum clearance and redevelopment. The war not only put an end to the rebuilding, but considerably increased the severity of the city's housing situation, as bombing reduced in number and condition the closely packed and densely inhabited houses in its central areas. It was felt that there should be no avoidable delay in providing the maximum number of homes for the many needy families, and considerations of design, layout and amenities had perforce at the time to be subordinated to this overriding purpose.

Building began in 1953 and was virtually completed by 1959. Government insistence on the maximum use of what was extremely good agricultural land led to a very high density of dwelling spaces, and this was to a great extent achieved by the construction of a large number of high blocks of flats. Ancillary buildings such as shops, pubs, and facilities for entertainment had to wait until the first wave of families in need were supplied with their homes. The full complement of schools was not completed until some time after these first arrivals had settled in. This situation has occurred in housing estates and in the early New Towns many times both before and after Kirkby's development. It has inevitably led to an exacerbation of the psychological anxieties and the social problems which accompany any large scale transfer of population from the highly sociable communities of densely packed city neighbourhoods to the quiet and the initial loneliness of a suburban estate. Kirkby was no exception, and some consider that the prolonged and single-minded concentration on housing there, which has only recently been relaxed, can be related to the unusually high incidence of vandalism and petty crime in the town.[1]

A plan of Kirkby today shows three neighbourhoods converging on a town centre with shops, banks, offices and a market. Neighbourhood centres provide local shops and primary schools. The four secondary schools, on the other hand, are not related to neighbourhoods. All are comprehensive, two for children of Roman Catholic parents only. But some such children attend the two County Schools: Ruffwood and Brookfield. The number of children attending Catholic and Anglican schools is almost equally divided between the two.

## II

In a survey of the town made by the University Department of Social Science in 1960, it was found that nearly two-thirds of Kirkby residents previously lived in the central or inner wards of Liverpool. Eighty-six per cent of the parents of Ruffwood children living in Kirkby had previously lived in this area, and altogether a larger proportion than on the estate generally came from the city. More than half of the estate households had been on Liverpool Corporation's housing list. nearly always becoming eligible for a Corporation house because they were living in over-crowded conditions. About one-third before moving to Kirkby had lived in rooms which would usually be entirely unsuitable for a family containing young children. Only about ten per cent had been provided with a house because they had lost their previous home through demolition or slum clearance, and about twice this proportion already had a Corporation house or flat in another district and had moved out to Kirkby by exchanging their accommodation. The remainder had moved on medical grounds or for one of a variety of other reasons.

As a result of the high proportion of ex-housing-list residents

[1] A new form of mobile police patrol, said to be based on methods used in Chicago, is held to be responsible for reducing remarkably the rate of crime and malicious damage in Kirkby in 1965. See the report in the *Liverpool Daily Post* dated 18 August 1965.

gaining priority through living in over-crowded conditions, the population of the town is very largely composed of young couples with growing families. While in Liverpool in 1961[1] one quarter of the population was under fifteen years old and fifteen per cent were over sixty years, in Kirkby nearly fifty per cent were under fifteen years old and only four per cent over sixty years (Table 2.1). Half the Kirkby households contained five or more persons in 1961,[1] and eighteen per cent contained seven or more.

TABLE 2.1. AGE DISTRIBUTION IN KIRKBY AND LIVERPOOL, 1961

| Age group (yrs.) | Kirkby Estate Per cent | Liverpool Per cent |
|---|---|---|
| 0–4 | 15 | 9 |
| 5–14 | 31 | 17 |
| 15–19 | 7 | 7 |
| 20–44 | 34 | 33 |
| 45–59 | 9 | 19 |
| 60 + | 4 | 15 |
| Total | 100 | 100 |

An age distribution of this character brings many problems, not least that families are usually moved to houses which will accommodate them suitably at the time, but with the arrival of more children will once more become overcrowded. In 1961[1] already twelve per cent of Kirkby households were living in densities of more than one and a half persons per room. There is at present, too, very little provision for children who marry and require homes of their own, although this situation is being improved by the efforts of the Urban District Council. Most newly married couples must still leave, however, and usually find rooms in Liverpool in their turn, thus starting the cycle once more. It is forbidden to share Corporation dwellings with other households, although at the time of the 1961 Census, seven per cent of households contained more than one family. This is not 'sharing' by strict Census definition, but probably represents married children living in with parents.

[1] Census information.

It also almost certainly underestimates the true position as many would not declare such a situation.

Over half the Kirkby households are either wholly or partly Roman Catholic. This is characteristic of the area from which most have moved where many of the families are Irish in origin. There seems little evidence that families of other denominations are appreciably smaller: large families are typical of the central Liverpool area where many previously lived, irrespective of religion. The 1960 Kirkby survey showed that among the seven per cent of families with six or more children, a slightly higher proportion were Roman Catholic, but among those with four or five children the proportion of Roman Catholic and non-Roman Catholic was almost the same.

About one-fifth of Kirkby residents live in flats and another five per cent in maisonettes. Most of the remainder on the estate are in semi-detached or terraced houses. The block flats are generally an unpopular type of accommodation and it was found in 1960 that significantly more flat dwellers wished to move (though not necessarily out of Kirkby) than those living in other forms of dwelling. Many no doubt took a flat because it was an improvement on their situation in Liverpool, hoping to be able to transfer to a house later. In fact it is very difficult to make such an exchange, few people taking such accommodation from choice, and this enforced immobility must increase the frustration of dissatisfied tenants.

## III

Kirkby at the present time is very much a one class town. Table 2.2 below shows the social class distribution of all Kirkby men in employment in 1961, using the Registrar General's classification of occupations, and compares it with Liverpool in the same year. The proportion of professional and managerial workers in Kirkby is very low indeed and non-manual groups generally are of a much smaller size in Kirkby compared with Liverpool. The proportion of skilled manual workers, on the other hand, hardly differs, but that of semi-skilled and unskilled workers is high.

TABLE 2.2. SOCIAL CLASS DISTRIBUTION OF EMPLOYED MALES LIVING IN KIRKBY AND LIVERPOOL 1961 (REGISTRAR GENERAL'S CLASSIFICATION OF OCCUPATIONS)[1]

| Social Class | Kirkby Estate Per cent | Liverpool Per cent |
|---|---|---|
| I and II | 4 | 10 |
| III (Non-Manual) | 10 | 16 |
| Total | 14 | 26 |
| III (Manual) | 39 | 37 |
| IV | 24 | 19 |
| V | 23 | 18 |
| Total | 86 | 74 |
| Grand Total | 100 | 100 |

Kirkby is some seven miles distant from Liverpool and the dependence of its wage earners on the city as a source of employment has continued. To a large extent this may be accounted for by the balance of skilled to semi-skilled and un-skilled male workers, for there are relatively few openings on the Trading Estate for the unskilled: most male employment is for men with some skill.

More than fifty per cent of employed Kirkby residents worked outside the Urban District in 1961 and each day about 13,000 people enter and 10,000 leave Kirkby on their journey to work.[1] This is obviously another source of dissatisfaction for it leads to much higher travelling costs than were experienced in Liverpool, where the docks and other employers of unskilled labour were close at hand.

Increased travelling costs and higher rents mean that the move to Kirkby has put an additional burden on the main wage earner who, if unskilled, may be on a low wage rate, or at least experiences wide fluctuations in take-home pay. This, and the unusually large number of openings for semi-skilled

[1] 1961 (10 per cent Sample) Census. See p. 17.

and unskilled women on the trading estate, may be expected to encourage those women able to go out to work to do so.

Approximately forty per cent of the total employed on the estate are women, mostly in processing and clothing manufacture. Thirty-four per cent of married women in Kirkby were in paid employment in 1961, but this includes some women without children. In the 1960 survey, 25 per cent of women living with their husbands and with children worked, 10 per cent full-time, and 15 per cent part-time. In a survey of the Crown Street area of Liverpool, that is the area from which many Kirkby families have moved, it was found in the summer of 1962 that 31 per cent of married women with children worked, in the proportion of 14 per cent full-time and seventeen per cent part-time; and in early 1963 that 26 per cent worked, eleven per cent full-time and 15 per cent part-time (Table 2.3).[1] These proportions are closely comparable to those found in Kirkby and the higher figure for summer may well be a seasonal fluctuation.

TABLE 2.3.  MARRIED WOMEN WITH CHILDREN IN EMPLOYMENT IN KIRKBY 1960 AND THE CROWN STREET AREA OF LIVERPOOL, 1962 AND 1963[1]

| | | Not Working | | Working full-time | | Working part-time | | Total | |
|---|---|---|---|---|---|---|---|---|---|
| | | No. | per cent | No. | per cent | No. | per cent | No. | per cent |
| Kirkby Estate 1960 | | 180 | 75 | 25 | 10 | 37 | 15 | 242 | 100 |
| Liverpool Crown St. area | Summer 1962 | 89 | 69 | 18 | 14 | 22 | 17 | 129 | 100 |
| | January–March 1963 | 84 | 74 | 12 | 11 | 17 | 15 | 113 | 100 |

It would seem probable that both in Liverpool and Kirkby, given the opportunity, those able and wishing to work do so, and that living away from relations, who in Liverpool might be available to mind the children, has not in fact affected the position. About half the mothers of children in the Ruffwood

---

[1] E. Gittus: unpublished data.

School survey worked. This higher proportion is no doubt because more of them than in the population generally have all their children of school age and are therefore better able to leave them.

The range of entertainments available for Kirkby families is naturally a good deal more restricted than it is in the city. The proportion of Kirkby residents going to the cinema at least once a week, for instance, had in 1960 dropped from 61 per cent while living in Liverpool to 16 per cent in Kirkby. An evening at the pub, or a dance or an afternoon at a football match were all less frequent occurrences after the move. Nevertheless, participation in local social activities organised by the church, clubs, political parties and so on increased significantly; 44 per cent of members of Kirkby households interviewed in 1960 took part in this type of entertainment, as compared with 31 per cent in Liverpool. The Roman Catholic Church in Kirkby is particularly active in this respect and provides licensed clubs at which many of their parishioners meet for a drink, a game of bingo or other amusement.

Two community centres are used for local dramatics, 'keep fit' classes and specialised interests of one kind or another. Clubs for teenagers and youth groups belonging to various organisations are available and will be considered in more detail in Chapter 8. Church attendance provides a basis for informal meetings among members, and this must be of particular significance to the large Roman Catholic population.

Kirkby therefore probably provides at least as many opportunities for local group activities as any other town of its size, for those willing or able to take part in this type of entertainment. Nevertheless, the town by 1960 had not yet emerged from the general malaise which invariably affects newly arrived tenants of suburban housing estates. Although a high proportion appreciated the change to a cleaner and healthier environment than they had previously experienced, and many were glad of the improved accommodation, two-thirds of the survey population still preferred their previous home, and nearly a quarter wished to leave the town. The two most frequently mentioned reasons given for preferring their old place of residence were more convenient shops and people's greater friendliness. It may well be that by the time of the Ruffwood survey, five years later, these particular grievances had disappeared, for additional shops had since been built and a certain familiarity with neighbours may be expected to have developed. Willmott has found in Dagenham that by the time the second generation of residents have grown up and formed families of their own, many of whom have in their turn settled on the estate, an emotional attachment has developed comparable to that in Bethnal Green before the original move took place.[1] Dagenham during its first years suffered from all the difficulties experienced by early Kirkby tenants: no shops, poor transport, little local employment and an emphahis on housing to the exclusion of all other development, leading to similar dissatisfactions among its residents. The first Kirkby tenants have been living there for thirteen years, and the first of their children who have married and now have their own families are being settled into houses built by the Urban District for this particular purpose. It may be hoped that with time a comparable adjustment to circumstances will take place in Kirkby to that which has apparently occurred in Dagenham as ties of family and friendship naturally develop.

TABLE 2.4. REGISTRAR GENERAL'S CLASSIFICATION OF OCCUPATIONS

| Social Class | Occupation |
|---|---|
| I | Professional |
| II | Managerial, semi-professional |
| III Non-manual | Clerical, commercial |
| III Manual | Apprenticed, skilled |
| IV | Semi-skilled |
| V | Unskilled |

[1] P. Willmott *The Evolution of a Community*, Routledge & Kegan Paul, 1963.

# 3

# *Ruffwood School—A General View*

*I*

Ruffwood is a large county comprehensive school with a twelve form entry designed for a total of 1800 boys and girls.[1] It is one of four such schools catering for the eleven plus population of the new urban district township described in the preceding chapter. Two of the other comprehensive schools are single sex and are controlled by the Roman Catholic Church; Brookfield, the second county school, is also mixed and is slightly the older foundation. Ruffwood opened in September 1959, two or three years after Brookfield. The latter was not, like Ruffwood, originally planned as a comprehensive school but was composed from two existing secondary modern buildings to which was added a third block. Ruffwood draws its pupils mainly from the north end of the township and for a time there was some degree of overlap with Brookfield's catchment area since it opened before its residential population had been fully accommodated. One result of this overlap has been that occasionally families have been split up, one brother going to one school and the other brother to the other school. Current school policy at Ruffwood, however, encourages the enrolment not only of siblings but also of groups of friends at primary school and even at street play-group level. It commenced as a nine form entry and gradually expanded from three hundred to its present nominal roll over a period of six years. The staff consists of some hundred full time

[1] The entry (1959) was of nine forms (300 pupils only. The entry has been as high as 460 pupils (sixteen forms) in some years. Numbers on roll have now, in the late 1960s, topped 2,000 mark.

teachers and about ten part-timers together with five secretaries.

The school has a fine campus and the visitor accustomed to the overcrowded and cramped layout of most inner city school buildings is immediately struck by the openness of the plan and the general spaciousness. Playing fields extend behind the school for some quarter of a mile. In addition to the cricket and football pitches there are tennis courts and a rural science department with various sheds and gardens and a number of livestock. To the south of the administrative building is an indoor swimming pool, and an open air theatre where plays and outdoor entertainments take place. The original gymnasium-cum-assembly hall is no longer big enough to hold the whole school population and this means that the school can no longer meet as a visible unit.

The main physical layout of the buildings follows the internal organisation of the school and is divided into three principal parts: the administrative offices, the classroom blocks and the house buildings. The main teaching is done in two multi-storey blocks while science and domestic subjects have their own buildings and the four houses are also located in separate blocks. Each house block has two staffrooms, one for the house masters and the other for the house tutors together with dining hall, activity rooms and locker space. There are some 250 boys and girls in every house and every age group is included. The girls are usually supervised by a senior house-mistress who acts as deputy to the housemaster. While each house operates as a unit, the very fact that in each building two houses share some of the facilities, such as dining room and staffroom, produces an inevitable tendency for the staff allocated to one block sometimes to think of themselves as, say, North or South Block rather than as Shakespeare or Shackleton House.

When the enquiry was made we heard many criticisms about the inadequacy of accommodation for members of the teaching staff in the house blocks. As their rooms were placed one on either side of the toilets they tended to be corridors between the main part of the house, and, as one of the teachers put it, 'Here we all are, sitting like in a railway carriage staring at each other.'

House teachers have private rooms (each room being shared by two house masters and two assistant house mistresses) which are used mainly for particular purposes, for example if a pupil needs to be seen alone. They are also used occasionally for house tutors' meetings but, in the main, house masters mix with other staff members in the common rooms.

Behind these staffrooms are the pupils' dining rooms.[1] Each of the four sections, East, North, South and West (comprising two houses each) dines in the main hall behind the staffrooms connected with the houses, and this involves double sittings. One house eats first one week and another the next week. In the canteens the tables seat eight pupils with one member of the teaching staff and here, as elsewhere in the school, there is a strong emphasis on social training.

## II

Ruffwood is organised on a modified version of what has come to be called the vertical system.[2] The division into houses for all social activities is crucial. In this way there is a complete mixing of ages, sexes and abilities. Brookfield, the other county comprehensive school already referred to, runs much more on a horizontal pattern with a breakdown in terms of ages. Its three building blocks are more or less organised into junior, middle and senior schools and the school is far more arranged by streams than Ruffwood. The latter streams in the sets but less tightly than in the more orthodox type of schools. The sets were streamed, at the time of our enquiry, as follows: (1) pupils of grammar school ability; (2) pupils of borderline ability between grammar school and secondary modern level; (3) those above average secondary modern level; (4) those below average secondary modern level, that is, the Newsom children; and (5) those definitely backward.

---

[1] These are also used for assembly, dramatics, film shows and social activities such as dancing and table tennis.

[2] See *London Comprehensive Schools, A Survey of Sixteen Schools*, published by the L.C.C., 1961, especially pp. 23-6 for a description of the two forms of organisation.

Stream Four, the Newsom children, were the largest of these five groups. This streaming pattern seems to have changed somewhat during the course of the school's development and growth, with at times only four main streams, at other times as many as six, but basically it seems that organisation into five streams is the normal system.

Pupils who have been consistently taught in the first and even the second of these streams may go on to a college of further education, college of education or to a university.

Stream Three comprises children who would probably take up skilled work, nursing and secretarial jobs; Stream Four tend to go into semi-skilled and non-skilled occupations, while Five, which is made up of children who have difficulty in either reading or writing, would be expected to get whatever low grade work happens to be available.

In 1959 when the school opened, the virtues of rigid streaming were generally assumed and Ruffwood at that time distinguished six levels of ability. There has been a gradual movement towards non-streaming. By 1967, that is by the time this report was in its final draft, only three levels were in operation, with well over half the total number of pupils in the middle band where they are taught mainly in classes each containing pupils drawn from a single house and instructed by teachers associated with that house. It is likely that the school will come down to only two levels within two or three years as the staff gain more experience of managing wide ability groups. The two levels will then be (a) normal, including the great majority of children, and (b) remedial, for children with communication difficulties (usually poor reading ability) or other special problems.[1]

Pupils are originally placed in sets according to their primary school test results in English, Mathematics, and Intelligence. In the first year, however, this is limited to Mathematics so that new pupils are taught mainly in stable groups.

The sets into which the school is divided for teaching purposes are not forms in the accepted sense of that word.

[1] This in fact happened and groups are deliberately mixed so that the first year comprises 8 parallel classes (each composed of children from one house) and 4 remedial classes each made up of pupils from two houses.

They do not have teachers put specially in charge of them with any pastoral responsibility. Theoretically it is possible but highly improbable for a child to be in the first stream for English but only in the fifth stream for Mathematics. It does in fact happen that a child can be in, say, the first stream for English, the second for Mathematics and the third for History or French. There is hence some degree of latitude available to accommodate pupils' strengths or weaknesses. Pupils are placed in the appropriate stream subject by subject and not, for example as might happen in an ordinary school, put in form 1a for all subjects because of their average performance. At Ruffwood they can be in what is the equivalent of 1a for History, 1b for Mathematics, 1c for Art, and so on. As a matter of fact, most children tend to be fairly consistently either near the top, in the middle, or in the bottom streams, as might be expected. This system allows some flexibility in the early years but, in the end becomes extremely rigid as transfers become more and more difficult to make because of the different work levels attained in the different streams. One major disadvantage, from the organisational viewpoint, is that very rarely indeed is one group of pupils found in the same place at any one time. The school timetable is extremely complicated as might be expected in view of the large numbers being dealt with and the amount of differentiation practised. It is no use, for instance, stating that John Brown is in 1a, because if he is doing Art he will probably be found in 1PX or whatever the case might be. On the other hand if he is doing Mathematics he might well be in 1a. The upshot of all this is of course that it adds to the general complexity of life in the school. The price of individualism may well, in a large comprehensive system, be an absence of group affiliations and consequent loss of strong in-group sentiments.

As the streaming system operated there appeared to be a more or less natural break between Three and Four, or, in other words, between the average and the above average. Pupils in the fourth stream did not take subjects such as Modern Languages; hence, once they were placed in Four it was extremely difficult for a child to move up to Three. Most teachers in the school referred to this phenomenon as the 'barrier' and much of the discussion at setting meetings, which were held every term, was centred on the operation of the barrier. It is no great matter if a pupil is placed in 1a or 1b for French because he can always move up into the higher grade if he shows particular promise, but it is very difficult for a pupil to cross the barrier, which thus acts as a very rigid and important distinction between academic groups.[1]

The school clearly faces a stiff task at the purely academic level. Almost all the 1959 intake who had previously attended Kirkby primary schools had taken the Cotswold Series II tests and the results showed general ability levels below the national average, which should be 100, as follows:

Verbal Intelligence 86
English 82
Arithmetic 87

While it must be said that this verbal intelligence test is designed to test suitability for grammar school courses and measured reasoning ability in a way likely to be considerably influenced by reading ability and by general knowledge, it still suggests that at that time the standard of attainment was at least a year behind the national average.

Even in the top set the figures were considered to be alarming:

Verbal Intelligence 104
English 97
Arithmetic 103

Serious questions were raised by these findings. Would the school have sufficient able children to set the pace for the others? Could an adequate fifth form course be provided when the number of pupils appearing capable of successfully tackling a full 'O' level G.C.E. course was so small? What were the prospects of producing a sixth form sufficiently large to provide economic teaching units for the staff and leadership and tone for the school as a whole? Could the school attract and retain

[1] The barrier was feature of a closely streamed system, but (1967) no longer exists in years I-III. The abolition of streaming footnoted on p. 21 has made much of this discussion now of merely historic interest.

staff of the highest academic quality without a greater proportion of more able children to teach?

We will consider these questions in the concluding section of the report but meanwhile would refer to the data regarding examination successes on p. 105 *et seq.* below as partially answering them in an affirmative way.

The 1960 and 1961 entries remained very much the same, due perhaps to the unsatisfactory staffing arrangements in many of the local primary schools. A further exacerbating feature arose from the fact that a few of the parents in the locality exercised their right to send their children, if of the appropriate ability, to grammar schools, while, at the same time, parents outside the district were later prevented from opting for Ruffwood. The presence in the school of a proportion, however small, who are attending as a result of parental choice must be a great boost to the school's morale. Parents living outside the school's catchment area seem to have chosen Ruffwood not merely for its academic level but also because of its good reputation for helping backward and retarded children.

A number of educationally subnormal children enter the school each year and the proportion remains high although there are signs of a slow improvement in this direction. (Table 3.1.)

EDUCATIONALLY SUB-NORMAL CHILDREN AT RUFFWOOD, 1959-1966

| Year of entry | Qualification for inclusion | Number | Per cent |
|---|---|---|---|
| 1959 | Reading age below 7·0 | 21 | 4·3 |
| 1960 | Reading age below 7·6 | 18 | 4·5 |
| 1961 | Reading age below 8·0 | 17 | 5·2 |
| 1962 | ditto | | 4·8 |
| 1963 | ditto | | 5·2 |
| 1964 | ditto | | 6·0 |
| 1965 | ditto | | 5·9 |
| 1966 | ditto | | 6·0 |

The school fortunately has a number of specialists in teaching backward children and in fact runs a special department devoted to this purpose.

The curriculum has been planned to meet the needs of all the children and not merely of the academically more able.

A degree of transfer between academic and less demanding courses exists but this is not to be thought of as the main justification for the school's existence. The main purpose is to extend all pupils to the limits of their abilities, not to produce an intellectual elite, and there is provision for a very wide range of interests and abilities. In the third and fourth year sex instruction is given to all pupils. This is by no means common in all secondary schools but is something that is well received at Ruffwood.[1]

One of the ways of assessing the school's success is obviously its performance in public examinations. But it is only one index and at Ruffwood advances on many other fronts are clearly of equal if not of greater moment. Of the 1959 intake sixty-six candidates secured one or more passes at G.C.E. 'O' level and of the 1960 intake the figure had risen to eighty-four. Of the 1959 group eleven gained passes at 'A' level in three or four subjects, six in two subjects, eight in one subject, and, in the same year, the school sent seven scholars to read for a university degree while nine entered colleges of education.[2]

## III

It has already been stated that the school was organised on a house system and at this point we might say more about this since it is the key to understanding the school's especial ethos and vertical organisation. Social education, discipline, administration and the general communication system depend almost entirely upon the house. The house loyalty cuts right across the teaching plan; and the academic system with its associated sets, divisions and streams, its syllabuses and its examinations seems to be somewhat separated from other fundamental aspects of the scholars' lives.

The essential unit in the house itself is the tutorial group. This is based on the year so that eleven year olds, twelve year olds, thirteen years olds and so on are in different tutor

[1] See p. 158 for data on parental attitude to sex instruction.
[2] These figures are incomplete as five of the 1959 intake were still at school at the time of writing.

groups, although there is a mixing of the sexes and of the abilities at this level. The tutor group meet together for about half an hour with their house tutor on most mornings of the week when registers are marked, dinner money collected, and announcements of various kinds made. They meet again for five minutes or so for registration at the beginning of afternoon school. The tutors are neither heads of academic departments nor house masters and so, in theory, are free to devote their undivided time and energy during tutorial sessions to gaining closer knowledge of the pupils and establishing mutual understanding and trust.[1]

Responsibility for the smooth and efficient running of house organisation lies on the shoulders of the eight housemasters. They are men and women especially chosen for the task.[2] They are also key people in a further respect: it is primarily their job to maintain contact with the home and the parents. The school's policy—in addition to running a kind of Parent-Teachers' Association suited to the peculiar needs discussed later in this chapter—is to invite parents to visit the school once or twice a year to meet housemasters and house tutors. This, of course, is in addition to inviting them to the various plays, concerts, and sporting events which are organised from time to time.

Much discussion has centred on the gigantic size of comprehensive schools and the consequent dangers of individuals being lost in a great sea of anonymity. Advocates of small schools stress the importance, especially in difficult neighbourhoods, of numbers being kept low enough to allow staff and pupils to establish face to face relationships and for all children to have someone to whom they can turn for help and advice.[3] Tutorial house groups are thought at Ruffwood to

[1] There is a particularly interesting account of the work of similar tutor groups as they operate at Forest Hill School, London, in *London Comprehensive Schools*, pp. 25-7.

[2] Posts as house leaders are open equally to men and women, although at the time this report was written seven out of the eight were men.

[3] In *Education and the Urban Child*, one of the authors of this report went on record in favour of such small schools in down-town urban districts such as Crown Street, but it is worth while pointing out that he was thinking at the time of an alternative not of comprehensive schooling but simply of much larger secondary modern units.

meet this problem satisfactorily. Their aim is to create groups small enough for the more reticent pupils to be brought into intimate contact with at least one member of the teaching staff who is especially charged with caring for them as persons. It further offers occasions for pupils to make personal friendships between one another and to do this, moreover, on a mixed ability and mixed sex basis. Such house groups are all the more necessary in a school like Ruffwood which, as we have already indicated, does not organise the day to day teaching on the traditional basis of forms. If there are not units to which pupils can be allocated small enough to permit close association to take place there is a very real danger indeed of some individuals, to say the least of it, feeling lonely and isolated to the detriment both of their school work and of their social and personal development.

It is interesting to note that only nine of the eighty-one teachers who answered our questionnaire considered that the children lacked adequate close contact with any one member of the staff. It is probable that the majority of children are in close contact with more than one of their teachers, although, as was pointed out to us, some types of children do not seem to be able to get on well with any of the teachers. But, for what it is worth, it is clear that the vast majority of the teaching staff do not consider that the factor of size precludes the establishment of reasonably personal relationships between staff and pupils.

Hence, not only are tutor groups crucial for house organisation at Ruffwood but in a very real sense the success or failure of much of what the school is striving to achieve depends upon their efficient operation. Here, of course, we are talking about the ideal situation in which tutors make the fullest possible use of their opportunities to get alongside their pupils and establish warm and sympathetic personal relationships. We are also assuming that the time provided in the timetable is adequate to achieve this objective and that other business does not crowd out the period available for more informal contacts. We felt that there was a real danger at times, however, that tutorial meetings could be overweighted by the collecting of money and the passing on of notices and general information to the detriment of the fundamental purpose for which they were established. However useful these meetings may be administratively, tutors need sometimes to be very wary not to allow more formal business to dominate the proceedings. It is, of course, always easier to deal with official school business and to pass on essential information than it is to cope with the often unstated and dissimilar personal needs of different boys and girls. Perhaps the chief value of these tutor groups resides in the fact that pupils may come to find through them sources of additional support in time of trouble or difficulty. However, the data given in the following table indicate that the housemasters are the first ones to whom the majority would turn.

In reply to the question, 'Which members of staff would you go to if you had a problem?', nearly half the children mentioned their housemaster, though a fifth said that they would not consult any teacher at all. The responses given are shown in Table 3.2.

MEMBERS OF STAFF WHO WOULD BE CONSULTED BY
RUFFWOOD PUPILS

| Member of Staff who would be consulted | Number | Per cent |
|---|---|---|
| Housemaster | 105 | 48 |
| House tutor | 30 | 14 |
| English teacher | 17 | 8 |
| Other teacher | 16 | 7 |
| None | 45 | 21 |
| No response | 4 | 2 |
| Total | 217 | 100 |

Although these answers are far from being conclusive evidence, they do suggest that there is a fair degree of contact and confidence between pupils and housemasters and tutors. Moreover, informal observation in the school supported this view. A very friendly attitude does seem to characterise pupil-staff relationships, far greater than is observable in many other schools. It may be that the youth of the staff and the fact that thirty-seven of the eighty-one who answered our questionnaire were unmarried, helped to this end, for young teachers without family responsibilities find it easier to take part in activities out of school, which we believe makes a significant contribution to the creation of good teacher-pupil relationships. Thus far, at any rate, the system seemed to work with a fair degree of success but we must not blind ourselves to the danger that merely arranging children in small groups is no guarantee that adequate personal contact between staff and pupils results. In fact the opposite could happen. A very great deal, as always, depends on the skill of the housemasters themselves in establishing a good house spirit and also on the tact and perseverance of the tutors in turning the bureaucratic intentions into human realities. This, to some extent, depends upon the successful operation of the system as a whole and upon the ability of the Headmaster to inspire in his colleagues the desire to make the comprehensive system work in every sense and not least at the face to face level in the relations between staff and pupils.

Housemasters undertake a certain amount of home visiting. This is not done as a routine but solely when they judge such a visit to be necessary. It is regarded as part of the housemaster's pastoral role that he should seek out the parents in cases of special difficulty rather than always invite them up to school. In this way a positive interplay between school and home life is effected, mutual confidence is established and invaluable information about a pupil's background is obtained. Each housemaster keeps complete records of the pupils in his house and the record cards are available for colleagues to read. Such a system makes for continuity and the amount of writing up involved is judged to be well worth while. Not only, should a housemaster leave, is useful information in this way handed on to his successor, but, furthermore, the very fact of having to make such records must assist the housemasters themselves to see their charges in the round, as it were, and in some developmental perspective and time scale. The keeping of records is not resented as just another clerical chore might be.

As we have already said, because of its size the school can never meet as a corporate whole and house assemblies have to take the place of school assemblies. Generally speaking at Ruffwood house assemblies are routine while once a week the groups of tutorials comprising perhaps two house blocks meet in the main hall for a larger assembly conducted either by the Head or by the Deputy Headmaster. We heard criticism of these larger assemblies from both staff and pupils. It is extraordinarily difficult to make morning assemblies of a spiritual nature fit harmoniously with the strains and stresses of running a disciplined establishment. The temptation to use part of the occasion for general pep talks or for harangues about various breaches of discipline is almost irresistible.

Either the religion becomes the conscripted handmaid of authority, in which case so much the worse for the religion, or else an atmosphere of temporary fantasy is created which has little relation to the real world in which people are required to operate different aspects of their roles during the remainder of the school day.[1]

## IV

This is perhaps an appropriate place to discuss the way in which the school operates as an authority system and to describe how communications between the various levels and layers take place. It contains, of course, an obvious hierarchy from the Headmaster and Deputy Headmaster downwards. A senior mistress takes special responsibility for looking after the welfare and discipline of the girls. In this way it is acknowledged that girls have different needs from boys and should be separately catered for.

The chain of authority within the school runs in two channels: and in some way separates the social from the

[1] It is perhaps not unfair and not entirely irrelevant to say that house assemblies were, on the whole, less criticised than more general assemblies, suggesting perhaps that the house system itself, because of its very success, assisted the creation of a sense of corporate unity. We must also say that, since our enquiry ended, the holding of assemblies in which hymn singing takes place has been discontinued as far as senior pupils are concerned.

academic, although, of course, the same body of teachers are simultaneously involved in both systems. One chain of command runs from the Head through the house system and influences other members of staff and pupils down the line. A second line of authority, the *academic,* is associated with those members of staff with special responsibility for subjects and known as heads of departments. The latter are not house-masters and hence are parallel authorities in their own right. It is perfectly feasible that subject heads who are responsible for the curriculum and teaching arrangements within their own specialisms may not be in complete sympathy with some of the *social* aims of the school. It is quite possible that they may consider that formal teaching time is being sacrificed to the social, recreational or informal parts of the programme. They may, in other words, be more interested in teaching History or French than in training people. This is, after all, an established aspect of the pedagogic role and one not to be denigrated. It is possible to see, however, that some degree of divergence of interest can arise between the two main types of teacher: the house staff primarily dedicated to social education and the subject experts primarily devoted to obtaining good academic results. The latter may be thought of as being subject-centred, the former more child-centred. These views need not necessarily clash or prove hard to reconcile. In some schools, grammar schools for instance, there need be no tension whatsoever between the two approaches. But in a school such as Ruffwood, with its strong sense of purpose operating at both the social and the academic levels simultaneously as integral parts of one and the same general policy, it is clearly a possibility that the two authority systems can collide.

We would emphasise, however, that this situation arose from the social structure of the school as well as from a clash of individual views or personalities. The actual geographical layout of the school also seemed to demand a fairly sharp differentiation of function between subject teaching and house organisations. We are arguing only from limited evidence, but it appears that a big school such as Ruffwood, inevitably demands some specialisation of function on the part of its staff.

All sorts of problems do in fact flow from the necessity to run a large scale institution along traditional authoritative lines. A subject head commenting on this in terms of discipline said:

> Much of the Head's authority is delegated to housemasters, heads of departments and others—as it must be. This is not always as effective as it should be, largely because it is difficult to be beastly to colleagues with whom one rubs shoulders so intimately in our tiny staffrooms, and one must be beastly from time to time to get things done.

This commentator seems to be implying that not only should heads of department be somewhat isolated from their junior colleagues but that housemasters should also be aloof. The majority of the junior staff were radically opposed to such a policy. Their often heard complaint which ran something like this, 'Abandon that bastion of privilege, that citadel of snobbery, the heads of departments' room', implied a much more democratic and egalitarian approach to the problem. We cannot adjudicate between these conflicting viewpoints, but would merely reiterate that they are indicative of difficulties involved in the organisation of a school of the size of Ruffwood. Such difficulties, arising from differentiation of role relationships in an institution where perforce the Head has to delegate much of his authority, are probably unavoidable without a drastic change taking place in the values of the system itself.

It is clear from the evidence we obtained that the institution of housemasters was extremely popular in the school both with the pupils and with the staff in general. It is also clear that heads of subjects were not so popular. This was more especially noticeable at the time of the survey than later when certain administrative changes were effected which made the position of departmental heads less invidious.[1] We certainly encountered a fairly widespread feeling of grievance centred

[1] That is, the abandonment of a separate staffroom for departmental heads.

chiefly, at the time, on the fact that the heads of departments
had their own staffroom. This, not unexpectedly, led to charges
of exclusiveness being made against the departmental heads
as a group, and to functional differences between members of
staff being overemphasised. Since housemasters as a rule did
not stay very long in their own rooms but mingled with more
junior members of staff in the often overcrowded staffrooms,
they were not exposed to this kind of criticism. But in our
view the hostility had other structural implications apart from
the fact that the heads of departments enjoyed their own
common room. It arose from the fact that the junior teachers
and the lower ranks in the hierarchy, as we have seen, were
responsible to two dissimilar immediate seniors in addition
to the Head and the Deputy Headmaster. They had responsibilities to the housemasters in matters of social organisation,
discipline and sport, and to departmental heads for all matters
of an academic nature. Such an arrangement is obviously
fraught with problems and could easily lead to frustration for
the teaching staff in general. Moreover, as another member of
the staff commented diplomatically: 'Some subject heads, who
are irreplaceable because of their skill and efficiency in their
own fields, are liabilities in other directions. They provoke
ill-feeling among junior staff and fail to see the importance
of social education. . . . They are not genuinely comprehensive
in outlook.' This latter point, that some of them are not
comprehensive in outlook, has the real sting in it. Another
younger colleague put it more bluntly. When asked what
improvements he would like to see, he said he wanted 'more
democracy and for some heads of departments to realise they
are in a comprehensive school and not at their last grammar
school'.

Comments such as those we have quoted above are more than
mere gossip. They are symptomatic of a divergence of outlook
and of differences of function which comprise one of the
school's basic problems: how, in fact, two often divergent views
of the task of education can be reconciled in one and the same
institution. Obviously members of the teaching staff are sensitive about their own status. While the Head's and the Deputy

C

Headmaster's positions are not challenged, there is some degree of concern if the middle range group of staff (the equivalent, perhaps, at university level of the senior lecturers) appear to arrogate special status and associated privileges to themselves. Such views and sensitivities may seem somewhat absurd to the outsider, especially to the outsider with experience in industrial and commercial organisations. But it is well to remember that teachers regard themselves as members of a learned profession, and anyone who occupies a position of greater responsibility within the school—the Heads apart—is usually thought of by established staff members as *primus inter pares* rather than as a superior officer. There is also, in many minds, the stereotype of the small school where only the Head is segregated from the others who meet in the same staffroom so that it seems virtually impossible to distinguish sharply between the different aspects of the teacher's role. Each feels himself to be responsible, perhaps through the Deputy Head, who is also a member of the common staffroom, to the Head for matters of discipline, for the organisation of out of school activities, examinations, matters affecting syllabuses or whatever. In a large school, however, it is much more difficult for a senior teacher to be involved in the day to day administration of a house and at the same time to organise the general teaching of a subject when there may be as many as fifteen junior members of the staff teaching that subject who have to be supervised in various ways.

This mainly structural and organisational problem may further be exacerbated by the fact that teachers who are academically oriented will, in the main, be steeped in the grammar school tradition which sees the function of education in terms of the transmission of knowledge and the socialisation of the young rather than as a method for achieving social change. This difference of outlook is clearly brought out in the answers to the questionnaire in which some junior members of staff commented on the 'snobbish' attitude of various department heads. The latter, so it appeared, with some notable exceptions, did tend to consider their junior colleagues as slightly inferior and frowned on the teaching innovations to which the younger staff occasionally resorted. We think that this kind of situation derives partly from differences of outlook as well as from the actual structure of the school system itself. We would wish, however, to qualify our comments here by making two further points. First, the criticisms must always be interpreted as being made against the heads of department as a group and not against specific individuals. It is probable that, as individuals, they are as popular or as unpopular as any other members of the staff. The two chairmen of the Teachers' Committee, for instance, were both at the time of our enquiry heads of departments. Second, we do not consider that the criticism we found can be simply accounted for by the usual senior-junior tensions which are to be met in any organisation. The housemasters are also senior teachers, often senior in grade to heads of department. It is usual for any disciplining of junior staff to be done, in the first instance, by their own housemasters. Yet the research workers never encountered any criticisms of them as a body of senior colleagues.

We have to ask ourselves why one group was popular and the other much more openly criticised. We think that physical isolation was probably the main precipitating cause of controversy, and that the fact that the subject heads met apart tended to accentuate these differences of outlook, between a more traditional and a less orthodox approach to the actual job of teaching, to which we have already referred. At the same time, we cannot ignore the difference of outlook on the part of the different groups comprising the staff as a whole, of which more will be said in a later chapter. Obviously there has to be a clearly defined line of authority in any school, and no teacher would desire it otherwise. Authority *per se* is not resented. It is mainly when authority verges on authoritarianism that the trouble seems to arise. A general democratic climate of opinion requires that authority be exercised after consultation and discussion have taken place, after individuals and groups have had an opportunity to express their particular viewpoints. This does not mean that a vote has to be taken or even that a general consensus of opinion must be implemented by those whose position in the hierarchy empowers them to make decisions and set policy. But it does come into conflict with isolationism, and the fact that housemasters had to mix with the rest of the teaching staff in the overcrowded house-block common rooms enhanced rather than lessened their authority by increasing their popularity and acceptability at the personal level. The result of this was that the social and disciplinary organisation of the school was supported by popular approval sometimes perhaps to the detriment of the academic organisation which was considered by many to be remote, undemocratic and exclusive. Thus what seemed to promote the rational efficiency of the school—the differentiation of administrative from teaching roles—tended to harm general morale and to make the system of communication, especially at senior level, less effective than it might have been.

## V

The fact that the school is spread out and is very large and divided into two main organisational streams makes communication both horizontally and vertically a matter of supreme importance. Considerable thought has been given to this over the years. Apart from formal staff or house or subject meetings, the main channel of communication is the Daily Bulletin. This consists of a duplicated sheet issued by the Deputy Headmaster every morning. In the early days this used to be pinned to notice boards but more recently it has come to be distributed to every tutor and its contents are supposed to be read out at house tutorial meetings. By this means the Head, and any member of staff for that matter, can bring the school's attention to any event or piece of news which may be of interest or general concern.[1] Some items are directed to restricted groups. For instance, information can in this way be passed quickly from teacher to teacher as well as from teachers to pupils. Not surprisingly the Headmaster himself finds this a most effective way for disseminating news or sending out

[1] See Appendix A for a specimen copy of a Daily Bulletin.

directives. As we have already suggested, tutors do not always find time to read out every item to their group and so information is occasionally blocked. In a smaller school where all can meet at morning assembly there is little danger of such a breakdown occurring. But it is clear that at a school like Ruffwood the whole system of communication depends to a very considerable extent upon each link in the chain doing its work effectively. Various other means have been considered. The installation of a tannoy system has been mooted to make communication more rapid and certain but so far it has been rejected on the grounds of impersonality and because it might make the school seem too like a factory. But telephones have been placed in all the houses so that the administration can ring through and get in touch with teachers immediately if the occasion should arise. The fact that the administration block is several minutes' walk away from some of the teaching blocks makes this an absolute necessity.

A particularly interesting feature of the school is the system of 'subbing': substituting for absent members of staff. With a large staff absences are fairly common. Moreover, the wide range of outside activities carried on by the school, the camps and visits to places of interest, and the fact that senior members of staff are given time off to make contact with parents, means that there can be as many as ten teachers away at any one time. The sub list, consisting of those who are expected to take the classes of absentee members of staff, is sent round to the house blocks before nine in the morning. The system works efficiently but because of its impersonal nature and the fact that it can mean the loss of coveted free periods produces a fair amount of mild criticism.

The Daily Bulletin and the sub list are important parts of the administrative system involving what was often disparagingly referred to as 'paper work'. Some of the junior members of staff thought that this was overdone by some of their senior colleagues to the point of being red tape. It is our impression that a great deal of written communication and recording is inevitable in the organisation of a large and dispersed school such as Ruffwood. It is something that teachers nurtured in a smaller and more intimate institution, may be apt to misunderstand and underrate in importance.

We have described the division of the school into five staffrooms, consisting of the four house blocks and the administrative section, and we have seen how the staff teach pupils frequently based on a different building block from themselves. The teachers, furthermore, have to act as links in the chain of communication between Headmaster and school, between subject heads and pupils and between pupils and housemasters—a most complex network that involves a great deal of paper work. Each tutor fills in forms of many kinds, makes many sorts of report during the course of the term, all of which have to be coordinated and despatched to the correct place at the correct time and dealt with in the correct way. In addition to reading out relevant information from the Daily Bulletin, the tutors record effort marks and merit marks, write out punishment slips, keep notes of lateness or absence, record pupils' promotion or demotion, keep examination marks and meal registers. All this can be further complicated by the failure of a pupil to attend at the right time or by the tutor's inability to contact a colleague who has given a pupil a punishment slip. It will be clear that the housemasters and heads of department have much more of this kind of work to get through than other members of staff and that the Headmaster and his Deputy are the most overloaded of all.

The reaction to paper work organisation may be as much emotional as rational, but for all that cannot be overlooked in any attempt to describe the life of the school. Some bitterness and frustration undoubtedly result from this aspect of the administration. The words of a junior member of staff sum up the typical attitude of the conscientious tutor:

Staff have to deal with too much administrative work. (However I am not sufficiently imaginative to dream up a way of overcoming this!) Tutor periods, ideally intended to foster relationships between staff and pupil, are far too often taken up with form-filling, list-making, or collecting money.

A senior teacher commented more tartly that 'an O. & M. consultant is needed to advise on ways of reducing returns and paper work, especially at the end of term.'

Complaints against excess (undefined) form-filling are probably unavoidable. So, too, is the paper work itself. It is inevitable in the organisation of a large institution. Clearly it is simpler and quicker, hence in the long run more efficient, if not so pleasant in other ways, to fill in a form which can be placed in the appropriate tray than it is to find a pupil or a colleague and have a face-to-face conversation.

## VI

Form-filling bulks large in the school's disciplinary system. Here again, teachers used to a more conventional arrangement may find the Ruffwood system irksome. A man accustomed to the direct punishment of offenders such as is still very common in many British secondary schools may find the form-filling of Ruffwood an irritating bureaucratic invention. One of the chief disciplinary checks is for the teacher to send the pupil to his or her housemaster who will then have a serious talk with the child. It is the expressed policy of the school to avoid corporal punishment whenever possible and to find some other form of sanction to meet the case. Housemasters, however, can and do use the cane when they consider it to be necessary and so too do the Head and Deputy Headmaster. Only 17 per cent of the teachers were against caning, although over half of those who accepted it qualified their approval. Many of these said that there was no alternative in a place like Ruffwood, although in principle they did not favour it. Others considered it suitable for boys but not for girls. But the kind of widespread and indiscriminate beating of children to be found in some schools[1] is forbidden at Ruffwood and, as far as one can see, this in general results in a happier and more effective school discipline. Parents themselves, however, were on the whole in favour of corporal punishment and sometimes even criticised the teachers for being too friendly with their

[1] See, in this connection, John Partridge *Middle School*, Gollancz, 1966.

pupils.[1] A weekly detention is also organised as a subsidiary disciplinary sanction.

The school is more concerned with setting a tone than with punishing defects. True to its general aim to promote social education, it 'does not regard its authority as ending at the school gates' and the Headmaster makes it plain that 'pupils bringing discredit on the school by their behaviour elsewhere, and particularly on their way to and from school, will be punished'.

The school also places a great deal of emphasis on outward appearances, manners, and general demeanour as adjuncts to its disciplinary code. House tutors are responsible for seeing that their pupils are properly dressed and conduct themselves in a becoming manner round the campus. Inspections of uniforms takes place when senior members of staff visit the houserooms to see that the pupils are correctly turned out. Boys wearing odd socks for instance are admonished. At an early date the school acquired its own uniform partly in order to develop pride in appearance and to foster taste in dress, but also 'to establish the status of the school in the neighbourhood and beyond'.

A certain amount of resistance to wearing the uniform has not unexpectedly been encountered from parents and from pupils. In the early years the staff had to exert considerable pressure to obtain the cooperation of parents in this respect but the evidence suggests that they have already won this particular battle quite handsomely.[2] By the end of the school's first year the Headmaster was able to report to the governors that 86 per cent of the school were wearing uniform, 'a considerable number having been helped by the local authority who paid the whole or part of the cost in cases of proved need.' Twelve months later the figure given in the annual report had risen to 90 per cent.

Teachers' attitudes towards make-up and nylon stockings varied considerably. Only eleven teachers out of the eighty-one interviewed thought that all the girls should be allowed to

[1] See p. 84 for documentation of this.
[2] See p. 82 for parents' exact views on the provision of school uniform.

wear nylons, but an additional thirty-nine thought that they were permissible for the senior girls. Thus two-thirds of the staff in all agreed to this. Only six teachers were against both nylons and make-up and nearly half, thirty-six in all, accepted make-up for seniors. One teacher's comment on Ruffwood's ban on nylon and make-up was as follows:

> The nylon situation at Ruffwood is ridiculous. Carried to its logical conclusion, the 'many girls would come with ladders, so no nylons' concept could be extended to 'many girls will come in dirty blouses so no blouses—certainly not white ones'. The use of discreet make-up could be taught practically to fourth year girls and upwards from day to day routine.[1]

Discipline is wherever possible based on rewards rather than on punishments. Merit marks are awarded for smart appearance, regularity and punctuality. There are in addition what are known as 'effort' marks. These are given in alphabetical terms (A to E) and are assessed by subject teachers. In this way quite moderately gifted children are able to score high effort marks and so are given some positive incentives to try hard to improve their own performance without the discouragement of constantly being compared with children of superior abilities. All such marks are collected by house tutors and entered in the terminal report books. The ultimate award of the school shield for work and merit to the most successful house is based upon these records.

Thus both losing and gaining marks for one's house are part and parcel of the general disciplinary system and help to reinforce other methods. The final sanction is a somewhat unusual one and involves the transfer of extremely recalcitrant pupils to a definite punishment set—analogous to the cells at a borstal perhaps—where they are taught by specially selected teachers in a special room and given very little communication

---

[1] An optional course in Fashion and Beauty is now available to fourth year girls. Moreover, there is now no ban on nylons and sixth form girls are free to use make-up. There is, however, an agreement that the Senior Mistress, if she thought it necessary, would speak to individuals about good taste in this matter, but this seems seldom to be found necessary.

with the rest of the school. This punishment set is mainly confined to the fourth year but it is occasionally possible for a third year pupil to be sent there if sufficiently disorderly. We found little criticism of this arrangement from the teachers, in spite of the obvious danger it involved of creating a new kind of high status anti-authority group within the school which might conceivably become a breeding ground for rebellion out of all proportion to its size.

A modified system of prefects and monitors is operated. As we have already seen, by the fourth year pupils know if they intend staying on for an additional two year course and those who decide to stay are put into the Four X group and those wishing to leave become the Four J's. The latter sometimes seem to feel that an invidious distinction is thereafter made between them and the Four X's, and the school has made an effort to overcome this by making members of the Four J's monitors or prefects. Some sharp criticism of this policy has been expressed by some of the pupils, and sixth formers seem to feel that it is particularly disagreeable for them to be expected to take much notice of these 'Four J types' who have virtually opted out of the school's main academic lifestream.[1]

## VII

One of the features of Ruffwood is its extensive programme of out of school activities. These are a definite part of the school ethos and it is clear that when members of staff are initially appointed they are made aware of the fact that the Head regards willingness to participate in one or more extra-curricular activities as an essential qualification. In addition to the usual sporting and athletic teams the school has at various times organised concerts and dramatic evenings, runs a choir and a recorder group and has a wide range of hobby groups such as woodwork, chess, stamp collecting, country dancing and gymnastics. There are German, mathematics and art societies, an S.C.M. group, and a social service group which first came into existence in 1961.

There is also a school club, staffed by the teachers, which

[1] There is now (1969) no formal prefect system. Instead all sixth formers have house or school responsibilities to carry.

meets regularly and offers every age group one evening a week of the usual programme of club activities, while on other evenings they can if they wish pursue special interests and hobbies. Although there is criticism of the fact that the club is arranged by years rather than on a more extensive membership basis (something which is a legacy from the conditions obtaining in its earliest days), it is appreciated by the pupils, and, as we shall see in a later chapter, is probably the most significant single leisure time activity for the Kirkby children who attend Ruffwood. At the school club the members can dance, listen to pop records, practice judo, swim, play tennis and indoor games and do almost any harmless or worthwhile activity in the company of their teachers. This latter point seems to us most significant. It is not only that the school as a corporate body thereby expresses its goodwill to the neighbourhood by attempting to make a contribution to the proper use of youngsters' leisure time, it is above all that members of the teaching staff give their time and energies entirely voluntarily, which in our view is of considerable importance. In the questionnaire for teachers we asked a direct question on this subject.[1] We asked whether they thought teachers should be paid for running out of school activities or if this should be regarded as an integral part of their vocation. The majority favoured the idea that this kind of activity should be voluntary and only fourteen were definitely of the opinion that it should be paid. A sizeable minority, however, were in favour of being paid in special circumstances, such as for running the youth club which involved a third session at school. But organising concerts, plays, hobbies groups and similar routine logical extensions of the normal school curriculum should be regarded as being part of the teacher's professional commitment. It would be misleading and starry-eyed, however, to suggest that there were no dissenters from this view or that complete unanimity reigned amongst the staff. We did find some who resented the pressure exerted on them to come back after school hours to direct these extracurricular activities, for whom even extra pay could not make it attractive.

[1] See Appendix B, p. 59.

The school year is punctuated by a round of excursions and visits, trips to the theatre, to museums, and outings in the countryside. It is impossible to list them all but an extract from the Headmaster's second report to the governors is worth quoting to give some idea of the scope and variety of these holidays and expeditions.

a. A visit to Paris and the Loire valley.
b. A caravan and minibus holiday on the south coast.
c. A visit to London, staying at an international students' hostel and making trips to places of interest.
d. A journey by canal barge from Llangollen to Manchester.
e. A walking tour visiting castles in North Wales and staying at youth hostels.
f. Youth hostelling tours in the Lake District and on the Isle of Arran organised in conjunction with Brookfield School.
g. House holidays in Snowdonia and Yorkshire.

In 1963 the school bought a disused railway station at Great Ormside in Westmorland. This is being developed as an outdoor sports centre on what are now fairly conventional Outward Bound lines. It is hoped that all members of the school will have at least one opportunity during their school life to spend a weekend at Ormside.[1]

More recently still, former scholars of the school have formed their own football teams and are now using the school playing fields at weekends. And members of the numerous and youthful teaching staff also organise their own round of recreation and social activities—dances, car rallies, hikes, amateur dramatics, and social evenings. Many of the unmarried members of staff take part in these gatherings, although, amongst some of the older teachers, there is the feeling that school and social life should not be mixed.

Altogether, it will be clear that a fair amount of activity goes on in the school grounds and buildings in addition to the daily routines of work and teaching. A school such as Ruffwood could in theory function as a social centre, if not for its entire

[1] See Appendix E for a fuller description of the work at the outdoor centre.

neighbourhood, at least for the past and present pupils and their families, and, as far as possible, an endeavour is consciously made in this direction by trying to associate the teachers with this Kirkby-based activity. At the time of our enquiry few if any members of the staff actually lived in Kirkby but more recently it has been found that close on a dozen are now living in the area and, should suitable accommodation become more widely available, it is possible that this number would increase. If this should happen there is no doubt that the school could become more and more a focal point for the social, recreative and cultural life of the locality. We see this as a natural result of the present policy which will make greater and greater demands upon the time and devotion of the staff and upon the willingness of parents and children alike to cooperate in what is an exciting social adventure.

Something of this may be seen, in embryonic form at least, in the work of the Friends of Ruffwood School Association, composed of teachers, parents, former pupils, and other friends of the school—about three hundred in all—which organises social activities for adults and, above all, seeks to raise money to purchase special equipment for the school. It so happened that while we were writing this section of the report an account of a major effort on the part of F.R.S.A. was reported in the Liverpool press.[1] This comprised the staging, in collaboration with the Lancashire Traction Engine Club, of a large scale transport rally at Haydock Park where something like twenty traction engines, eighty vintage cars and a number of early aircraft were on display. Pupils toured South West Lancashire to advertise the show and, when interviewed by the press, the school's Head Boy talked in terms of raising £3,000 for the Ormside outdoor centre. Much of the drive and leadership for this and for similar efforts of the F.R.S.A. inevitably come from the teachers—a further demonstration of the crucial part they are constantly being called upon to play in serving and shaping Kirkby's future.

[1] See *Liverpool Daily Post*, 13 July 1966.

# 4

# *Research Methods*

Three chief sources of information were used for obtaining the data on which this report has been based. These are respectively: —

a. answers to prepared questions given to the teaching staff, 4th form pupils, and the parents of children interviewed;
b. documentary evidence such as school records and reports;
c. personal observation by members of the research team, together with a great many informal talks and conversations with individual teachers and pupils.

We also conducted several open meetings when all members of the staff were invited to meet the research team to raise questions of interest, to suggest subjects for further enquiry and to discuss our eventual findings. These gatherings proved to be extremely valuable in a variety of ways.

As a general background, as we explained in Chapter Two, use was also made of material gained from a survey of Kirkby made in 1960, supplemented by data from the 1961 census.

By far the most important source of material was obtained from analysing answers to the three questionnaires, all of which are printed in the appendices.[1] The first of these, that directed to the teaching staff, was conducted at the end of the school session in July 1964. Table 4.1 outlines the response obtained.

[1] See Appendices B, C, D, pp. 127-152.

TABLE 4.1. RESPONSE OF SCHOOL STAFF TO QUESTIONNAIRE

|  | Male | | Female | | Total | |
| --- | --- | --- | --- | --- | --- | --- |
|  | Completed | Refused | Completed | Refused | Completed | Refused |
| Senior | 15 | 5 | 5 | – | 20 | 5 |
| Junior | 41 | 6 | 20 | 5 | 61 | 11 |
| Total | 56 | 11 | 25 | 5 | 81 | 16 |

Ninety-seven questionnaires were sent to the full-time members of staff of the school, together with a letter giving assurance of complete confidentiality and a stamped addressed reply envelope. Since we had only just begun our survey and wanted information about problem areas, we deliberately left many of our questions open-ended. Rather than set out a complete schedule demanding definite answers, we framed our questions so that we might gain information about the running of the school and left it open to the teachers to give fairly general answers to the topics which we raised.

We felt that this was the quickest way open to us to find out exactly how the school worked. As a result of our method of approach, many of our findings are based on material that may not be entirely representative, through incomplete coverage. Nevertheless, we think that it does provide us with pointers to areas of fundamental importance if the nature of the teaching profession is to be understood and sociological analysis of the British educational system further developed.

The response of the teaching staff, 84 per cent,[1] was, in our opinion, poor. This was moreover despite the support of the hierarchy and despite the fact that one of the research workers had been teaching in the school during the preceding term. There is no doubt in our minds that the teachers had a deep-seated reluctance towards filling in our questionnaire, in spite of their own friendship with some of the research staff. This seemed to stem from many causes. Firstly, perhaps, it came from a fear that the research team was secretly in league with the authorities; this fear we successfully overcame in the end,

[1] By November 1964 when we closed the survey. It was necessary to continually remind the teachers during August to November.

but it accounted for some of the early delay. Secondly, the questionnaire appeared to some minds to be unduly long. Thirdly, ten out of the sixteen refusals were from teachers of subjects in which little writing or theorising were necessary, and in many ways we felt that they found it difficult to frame written answers to some of our more open questions. Only in one case, however, was there any expressed hostility to the survey as such.

Many of the eighty-one respondents, however, obviously filled in the questionnaire with considerable care and thought, and we felt that what we lost in quantity we certainly made up for in quality.

Although we decided that the main weight of our enquiry should fall upon the teachers, since they formed the body most able to supply informed answers to the questions with which we were mainly concerned, we decided that their views should be balanced by additional surveys of older pupils and their parents. The parents, we thought, would help to reveal how far the policies of the school and its teachers had penetrated and been accepted by the local community.

We elected to interview children in the fourth forms, because this is the stage at which they must make up their minds either to leave or to remain for courses which can prepare them to take G.C.E. at both ordinary and advanced level. At this point, if at any time, the pupils must give some thought to their future and their attitude may reasonably be expected to reflect the balance between school and home influence, indicating how far these are in conflict and how far they have become reconciled.

The pupils were assembled in relays in the main school hall and were given the questionnaires under the supervision of at least two staff and two of the authors. If help was needed the child raised his hand, and one of the authors would go to him. No communication at all was allowed between the children themselves, and this was strictly enforced. This method ensured a hundred per cent response! The questions were designed to investigate, in relation to both parents and children, the following four main points: —

1. The attitude of an almost exclusively working-class community towards the type of education provided at Ruffwood, and in particular the interest in using the educational opportunities offered by the school in excess of the minimum requirement.

2. How far the school's policy relating to education, the relationship between pupil and teacher, and, in the words of the Headmaster in his first report to the governors, the acquisition of 'self respect, ambition for material and cultural advancement and a sense of responsibility and obligation to the community' have succeeded.

3. Opinions as to where the division of responsibility should lie between home and school in the child's development and training.

4. How far the town of Kirkby provides for the extracurricular activities and interests of the school child.

The questionnaires are given in full in the Appendices. It will be noted that in many cases the same question was asked of both parents and child. Such questions were mainly related to the first category above and included their opinion on the value of extra time at school and in training, and the type of job hoped for. Dual questions also related to attitudes towards Kirkby gangs and vandalism, opinions on what facilities for younger people are required in Kirkby, and what proportion of children expected to remain in Kirkby when grown up whose parents also wished for this.

It was administratively easier to give the pupils' questionnaire to all fourth formers in the school and to take a sample after their completion, than to select a sample of pupils first, who would need to be taken out of class separately and would require additional attention from staff.

The questionnaires used were those completed by pupils from four of the eight school houses. The houses provide a complete cross section of all sets in the school, where the only selection relates to the inclusion of siblings and known friends at the school previously attended. The first did not affect the sample; the second might just conceivably have marginal effects, but we did not consider that they would be significant. As the child's records are kept on a house basis, this method made the provision of information relating to the pupils less laborious for the authorities than if a random sample of all pupils had been taken.

This resulted in 227 pupils' questionnaires and was followed by interviews with parents of survey children. These were conducted by 2nd year Social Science students, superintended by one of the authors. There were ten complete refusals giving a 96 per cent response from at least one parent. Five refusals were from parents of girls and five from parents of boys. Most of those who refused were aggressive and may well have had opinions and attitudes towards the school considerably more hostile than those of parents interviewed.

Where it was possible to interview only one parent, the record was included. Husbands were responsible for most of the gaps in parents' responses, not always by refusing to answer, for often in spite of many calls the interviewers had no success in finding the husband at home. There were only two wives who refused but whose husbands gave interviews. Table 4.2 gives the number of families where only one parent was available, with the reasons for this.

Of the 217 pupils finally included in the survey, 119 were boys and 98 girls. Table 4.3 gives the number in each of the five school sets by sex. All except thirteen lived with both parents, two of these thirteen living with one parent and one step-parent, and the remainder with one parent only.

The way in which the questionnaires were administered ensured that as far as possible there was no interaction between parents and children while the questions were being answered. Certainly this was so as far as the children were concerned, but in some cases it was inevitable that the child who had taken part in the survey was present while the parents were interviewed. In fact, this occurred in nearly one third of households while one or both parents were interviewed, and it is difficult to know how far it would affect the responses of the parent concerned. If it did so at all, it is expected that the total result will be small, but this is a possible source of bias which cannot be evaluated.

Nearly all questions asked of parents required separate answers from the husband and wife, and in half the households in the survey husband and wife were interviewed together. Here again it is impossible to guess how far the responses, or even the presence, of one affected the other. However, it was considered that this possibility was a risk which must be taken, for the alternative of asking for a separate room to interview each partner on his own was likely to result in large scale refusals.

TABLE 4.2. RUFFWOOD SURVEY PARENTS BY HOUSEHOLD STATUS AND RESPONSE

| Household Status | Number Interviewed | Refusal or no contact | Total |
|---|---|---|---|
| Both parents ⎰Husband | 180 | 24 | ⎱ 204 |
| living together ⎱Wife | 202 | 2 | ⎰ |
| Widower | 2 | — | 2 |
| Widow | 3 | — | 3 |
| Divorced or separated mother | 6 | — | 6 |
| Father and stepmother | 1 | — | 1 |
| Mother and stepfather | 1 | — | 1 |

TABLE 4.3. RUFFWOOD SURVEY PUPILS BY SEX AND SCHOOL SET

| Set | Boys | Girls | Total |
|---|---|---|---|
| 1 | 16 | 15 | 31 |
| 2 | 16 | 19 | 35 |
| 3 | 29 | 26 | 55 |
| 4 | 47 | 37 | 84 |
| 5 | 11 | 1 | 12 |
| Total | 119 | 98 | 217 |

Where it has seemed appropriate, a 'chi-square' test of significance has been applied to the data. When a significant difference is noted in the text this infers that the probability of such a difference occurring by chance is less than 5 per cent.

Finally, we would argue that taking into consideration the limited manpower available and the fact that the three main research workers were all committed throughout the period of the research to university teaching and various associated academic chores the combination of methods of enquiry outlined above enabled us to get a fair and objective picture of the total life of the school in question. It may well be that there are things going on that we missed, and that we occasionally failed to grasp the significance of what we saw or heard. But the frequent formal and informal contacts we had with various members of staff helped to offset such sources of weakness. Moreover, the fact that one of our number over a period of several weeks taught groups in the school, had the freedom of the staffroom and was able to observe a great deal at first hand enabled us, we believe, to evaluate the answers to our questionnaires without the dangers of excessive naïvete and without the charge of relying solely on second hand experience being brought against us. We would point out that our association with the school covered in all a period of some three years and we were thus permitted to have something of an inside view of how institutional changes in a school take place and, above all, what their consequences are in relation to its aims and objectives.

# 5

# *The Teachers*

## *I*

As we said in the preceding chapter, the main weight of our enquiry was directed towards the teaching staff because we felt that they were not only more articulate than parents or children but that their role was in many ways the most crucial. The success or failure of any school, we believe, depends to a tremendous extent upon the quality of the staff and the degree to which they align themselves positively with the policy laid down by the controlling body and by the Headmaster in particular.

Table 4.1 in the previous chapter[1] has given the composition of the members of the teaching staff who cooperated with our enquiries. The criterion of seniority which we took was that of a head of department allowance, since this was the generally accepted view of the staff. People with graded posts, therefore, who may well have been earning more than a junior head of department, were classed for our purposes as junior. It will be remembered that there was a head of departments' room which at one time segregated them from the rest of the school; this seemed to justify our selection of seniority.

A higher proportion of men than women occupy the senior positions (though among respondents the disproportion is less marked), and they have a tendency towards being better qualified in terms of the possession of a degree or qualification of degree status, over half having a degree as opposed to about one third of the women.

[1] See p. 47.

The age range of the teachers in the school was decidedly young, and this was thought to have a definite connection with its ethos and achievements. Forty-eight of our informants were in their twenties, only one of whom was a head of department; twenty-five were in their thirties and only eight were over forty. It is possible that older teachers did not find either the school or the area quite so attractive and therefore did not apply, or left as soon as they could.

The social class of origin of the teachers, as determined by their parents' occupation, is given below.

TABLE 5.1. SOCIAL CLASS OF RUFFWOOD TEACHERS' PARENTS

| | Age Group of Teachers | | | |
|---|---|---|---|---|
| Social Class[1] | 20–29 yrs | 30 yrs & over | Total | Per cent |
| I & II | 24 | 12 | 36 | 44 |
| III | 18 | 18 | 36 | 44 |
| IV & V | 4 | 3 | 7 | 9 |
| None, retired | 2 | 0 | 2 | 2 |
| | 48 | 33 | 81 | 100 |

The school was recognised by the teachers themselves firstly as a tough assignment or a challenge, and secondly as a stepping stone to future promotion, both of which facts might tend to discourage older teachers (who perhaps had already got their promotion) from applying. Another factor governing the age range was the rapid rate of turnover in the school, which appeared to be a result of promotion to positions in other schools. Of the ninety-seven teachers answering the questionnaire in June 1964, only fifty-six remained at the school in September 1965. Forty-six of the staff moreover had no teaching experience prior to taking up appointments in the school.[2] Undoubtedly a young staff can create problems for the hierarchy in terms of discipline and technique, yet without doubt one of the main reasons for the school's impact on the locality was the youth and enthusiasm of the staff. In many

[1] Registrar-General's Classification of occupations.
[2] It must be pointed out that the school had only been open five years.

ways they were able to teach in a challenging environment free from the ties of tradition which often affect the grammar school teacher. They desired to change the system, not to confirm it, and in this they were greatly encouraged by the senior staff.

Although many of the teachers did appear to have this pioneering zeal, it must not be thought that they were of predominantly working class origin or outlook. Thirty-six of them came from professional or managerial background, the same number from skilled background, and only seven had fathers in the semi-skilled and unskilled categories. Thus 44 per cent were of middle class origin, while *de facto* by their occupation as teachers they were themselves all of the middle class. When we contrast these figures with those for the parents of the children we find that only 4 per cent of these were in the first two categories.[1] Thus, in terms of the Registrar-General's socioeconomic scale, we have a predominantly middle class group of teachers educating predominantly working class children. We shall see later that this problem, that of alien standards and values between teachers and pupils, was very much to the forefront of the teachers' own assessment of their problems.


## II

Turning to the organisation of the school, we asked a number of questions which gave members of staff an opportunity to vent grievances. From these questions we gained information, firstly regarding specific objections, and secondly regarding the attitude which members of staff had to the school. On the basis of their answers we divided up the respondents into those who expressed some definite criticism of certain important aspects of the school, those who expressed a definite satisfaction with the school, and those who remained neutral (on paper at least). (Table 5.2.) Certain points must be made here. First, it is obvious that criticism may be strong and yet

[1] 1961 (10 per cent Sample) Census. See Table 2.4, p. 17.

the critic may prefer working in his school rather than in any other; the Headmaster himself and many of the responsible policy makers in the school were strongly critical of some aspects of the school life. Criticism expresses concern as much as condemnation. Secondly, as a result of one rather loaded question which was introduced in order to encourage members to air their views, it is likely that a much larger proportion were found in the critical section than might otherwise have been the case. The answers we received are, therefore, suggestive, but must be treated with caution.

TABLE 5.2. TEACHER'S ATTITUDE TOWARDS RUFFWOOD SCHOOL

| Attitude towards school | Senior teachers | Junior teachers | Total | |
|---|---|---|---|---|
| | | | Number | Per cent |
| Critical | 5 | 26 | 31 | 38 |
| Neutral | 4 | 20 | 24 | 30 |
| Favourable | 9 | 10 | 19 | 23 |
| Uncodable | 2 | 5 | 7 | 9 |
| Total | 20 | 61 | 81 | 100 |

Not only are junior staff less likely to be satisfied with the school, but there is a tendency, though less pronounced, for the younger staff also to take this attitude, twenty-one of the thirty-one who put forward complaints being in their twenties. It may be that some of the criticisms arose as much from the healthy enthusiasm of young teachers as from any profound dissatisfaction on their part about the running of the school.

At the same time it appeared that teachers who were in sympathy with the policy of the school and who felt a definite concern to help the children of the neighbourhood were less critical or more in favour of the school than those who were out of sympathy with the pioneering aims of the Headmaster. For instance, none of the few teachers who disagreed with comprehensive education gave any praise to the school, and significantly fewer of those critical of the school favoured comprehensive education. The hierarchy laid strong emphasis on the social side of teaching in the neighbourhood, and it is noticeable again that, although there were only three teachers who disagreed with this policy, all of these were dissatisfied. Of the minority group of teachers (twelve out of eighty-one) who thought that the size of the school was a definite hindrance, ten passed adverse comments, while significantly more of those in favour of the school believed that the size allows greater scope and variety.

When we look at the attitude of the staff to the children, again we find that significantly more of those finding the children generally cooperative were satisfied with the school. These results might suggest that closer attention could be paid to attitudes of staff in relationship to policy, type of school, and neighbourhood when appointments are made. No doubt forms of pre-selection and selection take place but it does appear that those members of staff who are most satisfied with the school are in greater sympathy with the aims and problems facing it. The Head and senior staff aim to provide a challenging education for the children of this new town. They tend to foster what is generally called a liberal or progressive approach. As we would expect, the staff who accept this challenge and are more in sympathy with the problems of the area are happier in the school. Other teachers, it appears, would have found a pleasanter environment in a more conventional school. If the policy of the school is in fact to modify the social system, then we may conclude that only those who feel a definite identification with such a policy are likely to be generally satisfied despite their criticism of organisational details.

In fact their criticism of such details may in some instances be regarded as an index of their general satisfaction with the major goals and objectives of the school and of the Headmaster.

## III

We also asked the teachers whether the size of the school was of help or hindrance. As one would expect in view of the difficulties surrounding the head of departments' room and regarding the paper-work involved, our responses to this question were by no means all favourable to this aspect of the school (Table 5.3).

TABLE 5.3. TEACHER'S ATTITUDE TOWARDS SCHOOL SIZE

| Attitude towards size | Number | Per cent |
|---|---|---|
| Helped (without qualification) | 23 | 28 |
| Helped (with reservations) | 13 | 16 |
| Helped and hindered equally | 22 | 27 |
| Hindered | 12 | 15 |
| No response | 11 | 14 |
| Total | 81 | 100 |

Thus it may be seen that the teachers are on balance not critical of the school merely on account of its size. Among those believing without qualification that the size helped were a slightly higher proportion of senior than junior staff. Why this was so, we can only surmise. It might be that the younger teachers are more realistic in their appraisal of what takes place in a school, or again it may be that teaching in a large school makes greater demands with consequent strain on junior than on senior staff.

It might be expected that significantly more of those teachers who are (a) in favour of comprehensive education, and (b) in favour of the school feel that a nominal roll of 2000 is not excessive. The most interesting results gained from the questions on size are those related to the attitudes teachers have to the children. Of the teachers who felt that the size of the school by and large helped, significantly more thought that the children were generally cooperative than had serious reservations with regard to it.

This tends to suggest that there is a group of teachers who are dissatisfied with the school for perhaps a variety of reasons. Their answers to many questions tend therefore to be similar. For example, if a teacher is dissatisfied with comprehensive education, he is more likely to (a) think the school too big, (b) be unenthusiastic about the school generally, (c) find the children uncooperative. The difficulty (and it is probably an impossibility) would be to find the primary factor involved.

## IV

On the questionnaire we asked four questions specifically relating to the curriculum. Since these involved complicated answers and since, in a sense, the answers given relate to the pedagogical side of the school rather than to the social we shall only briefly deal with the comments made by the teachers.

In answer to a direct question as to whether any sections of the pupils were being overlooked, very few teachers said the brighter children were being overlooked but nearly half said that they had guilty consciences about the third quartile[1] and backward children. It is difficult to say how valuable these comments were since it had become fashionable after the Newsom Report to consider the below average child as most in need of help and attention. As one teacher commented:

> It is hard to find staff who want to teach those just above the remedial classes. The academic want to teach academic streams; the progress[2] department are trained to teach backward groups. This group are in a 'no man's land'.

Another aspect of this difficulty was seen in the division of the school into five ability ranges: the first and second being theoretically at any rate academic, the third being above average, fourth below and fifth remedial. The big division was seen between the third and fourth ability groups and it was difficult for reasons of subject and of time-table to transfer between these levels. In response to a question concerning the organisation of the school one of the staff wrote: 'Educationally the block which exists between levels 3 and 4 is a bad thing. It is *said to be* impossible to organise the school any differently. If this is so then this is a major fault of the comprehensive system.'

Some of the senior and a few junior teachers (eighteen altogether) believed that the only way to avoid penalising these third quartile (Newsom) children was to bring in some

---

[1] Below average children who are not in the bottom, or 4th, ability group.
[2] Remedial.

limited form of non-streaming. It was interesting in that this desire to experiment with non-streaming appears to be strongly correlated with a certain type of teacher. As we have shown above and will discuss later, certain types of teacher saw the school as an instrument of social change (social justice, they would probably call it). It appears that these teachers, refusing to believe as they did in any rigid social hierarchy, were also prepared to bring democracy and equality right down into the classroom.

None of the fifteen teachers who appeared to find the children uncooperative and none of the twenty-nine who answered 'Yes' to caning, without any reservation, were in favour of experimentation with non-streaming. In addition there was a strong relationship with political opinion, significantly more Labour supporters than those of other parties wishing to change the traditional ability streams.

The evidence that there was in the school a type of 'reformist' teacher becomes even stronger when we look at the general views of the non-streamers. Significantly more of those teachers opposed to streaming than those who supported it[1] were graduates, teaching 'Arts' subjects, who were in favour of comprehensive education, desired to work towards some kind of classless or at least more equal society, and who, in reply to a question as to the aims of the teaching profession in a working class district, not merely said that they wished to raise standards, but rather stressed the importance of maintaining some aspects of both middle and working class values.

Here then we see a minority group, who wished, within the limits imposed by the examination system at one extreme and by the fact of backwardness at the other, to try to educate children of all abilities in the same class room. We do not intend to enter into the argument regarding streaming, but the fact that this group of teachers existed who also appeared to have similar views on other subjects supports our thesis that this type of school tended to attract staff committed to

[1] This does not mean that a majority of either graduate or Arts teachers were in favour since there were only eighteen teachers who wished to experiment with non-streaming.

social reform. Rather than accepting the hierarchical values of the social system, they wished, to some extent at any rate, to provide at least an egalitarian approach in the school.

There was a strong emphasis by the staff on such items as social training, camping, holidays at Great Ormside, music, drama, visual aids, films and sport. With the exception of the last, these would hardly be the traditional activities stressed by teachers of, say, a typical grammar school. Here again we see an attempt to break away from the traditional types of teaching in the interests of the children whom the staff often felt were underprivileged. One teacher, and he was not alone, suggested the 'scrapping of the classroom organisation and a greater drawing on stimuli from new environments outside—visits, camping, films, the theatre.'

## V

Naturally we asked questions regarding pay and tried to elicit the teachers' thoughts about this thorny subject. We had expected that one of the main bones of contention was the question as to whether teachers should be paid for voluntary activities or not. As we saw in chapter three the teachers were expected to put in at least one night per week after school in helping to run a society or one of the school youth clubs. Sometimes they were expected to give up a Saturday or Sunday to help organise an outing or a camp. In the main the staff accepted the organising of extra-curricular activities as part and parcel of their job for which, within reason, no extra pay was required.

To the direct question regarding salaries we obtained a great variety of responses. It will be readily believed that few were satisfied (ten out of eighty-one). (Table 5.4.)

Most teachers believed that they were badly paid, but they adduced different arguments as to why this was the case and why they should receive more. Among the main factors mentioned were the distinction between graduate and non-graduate salaries, and the difficulties which a young male non-graduate teacher had, especially if he was married. We

TABLE 5.4.  TEACHERS' ATTITUDE TO PAY

| Attitude to Pay | | Number | Per cent |
|---|---|---|---|
| Adequate or fair | | 10 | 12 |
| Poor; criticisms relating to: | | | |
| (a)  status etc, | 9 | | |
| (b)  graduate distinctions | 6 | | |
| (c)  other differentials | 3 | | |
| (d)  starting pay | 8 | 55 | 68 |
| (e)  inadequacy for married men e.g. length of scale. basic rates etc, | 14 | | |
| (f)  non structural factors | 15 | | |
| Suggestion of efficiency bar | | 7 | 9 |
| No response | | 9 | 11 |
| Total | | 81 | 100 |

intend to make only one or two comments regarding pay since this is well out of our field. There is, however, no doubt that a young male married non-graduate teacher who earned £600 and £700 per annum was in a serious financial situation. It would, for instance, be almost impossible to get a mortgage and in addition the length of the basic scale offered him little immediate relief. On the other hand, to take extremes, a young graduate unmarried woman, who probably did not intend to remain in teaching for long, would be quite well placed.

This brings us to the general question of the structure of the teachers' salary scale. Our respondents showed two marked differences of opinion on this issue.

One school of thought was violently opposed to differentials; this is the egalitarian group who felt that competition for posts was inimical to teaching as a profession. One teacher, a head of department, wrote:

> The present structure of pay stinks. We have embarked on a pay scheme which sets teachers perpetually on the move and causes envy and invidious comparison within the profession.
>
> Which head of department is worth £580 p.a. more than one of the teachers in his department? It is scandalous. It smells of the opportunity state where competition and the rat-race are all that is understood.

The opposite point of view implied that the teaching profession should be made more financially competitive and drew comparisons with industry. These two view-points represent differing persuasions and we rate them as being of special interest in the setting of a comprehensive school as such.

Graded posts involve a peculiar type of promotion. In the teaching profession, below the rank of head, or deputy, there are two avenues of promotion; the first is that of head of department, the second is that of graded post. The interesting factor here is that heads of department are usually appointed to do a specific job whereas graded posts which are *de facto* in the gift of the head do not relate to a definite position. Thus difficulties arise between teacher and teacher, and teacher and head.[1] This can happen in any school and Ruffwood is no exception. Naturally enough a headmaster tends to offer graded posts to colleagues who go the 'extra mile' with him and with the school.

## VI

We have argued that conflict between school and home is to some extent implicit in an area such as the one in which our school was situated. We do not believe that the conflict at Kirkby is nearly as clear cut as in a situation where the parents are actively hostile to education and teachers. Rather the difficulties seem to arise from inadequate communication. It appears from the parental questionnaires that the children's fathers and mothers are in favour of the school in particular and of comprehensive education in general. When we look at the teachers' answers, however, we begin to notice the gulf between what the school is trying to do and the teachers' assessment of the attitudes and aspirations of the neighbourhood. Without passing any judgment either way, we maintain that the school's policy of reform is a precipitating factor in this conflict situation. It is only by understanding that reform

[1] One head teacher in a smaller school than the one we studied commented on a question regarding any reform he would like to see in his school: 'A dining room and the abolition of graded posts'

implies change and change implies some element of conflict that we can hope to explain the working of a school of this type in relationship to the community it serves.

By and large, the teachers were critical of the parents of the children. By this we mean that they made comments about home background or the difficulty of educating children when there was little cooperation or understanding by the children's parents. Fifty-one of the eighty-one teachers made some such critical remark whereas only seven seemed definitely favourable to the parents as a group. Twenty-three were neutral or made no response to the relevant question.

The opposite picture, however, emerges when we look at the teachers' attitude to the children. Forty-eight found them, by and large, cooperative, fifteen uncooperative and eighteen made no comment. There was, however, a marked tendency for teachers who found the children cooperative to be less critical of the parents also.

There does appear to be a relationship, remarked upon before, between attitude to the school's policy and attitude to children and parents. Given that the parents were generally criticised and the children praised, these teachers who were in favour of comprehensive education tended to be less critical of both groups. This was also true of those teachers who saw a moral difficulty in their role as teachers in a working-class community, whereas those who merely wished to raise standards and saw no problems about imposing alien values tended to be more critical of both children and parents. Again, as we should expect, the teachers who praised the school, who were in favour of some non-streaming and felt that the size of the school was more of a help than a hindrance, also tended to hold a more favourable attitude towards parents and pupils.

We are not trying to argue that any of these factors by themselves exert profound significance, but taken together they show that those who were in favour of the school's progressive policy tended to be slightly more sympathetic to the parents and to find their children more cooperative than the more orthodox group of teachers.

Whether or not the teachers were critical of parents or

pupils, it is certain that all of them, progressive and orthodox alike, saw very real difficulties in educating children, due to the local environment and its social history. On the teachers' questionnaire we asked a question about the advantages and problems of education in the locality. *More and longer comments were written on this than on any other question.* Let us try to summarise these responses.

By far the majority of answers related to the problems; only fourteen answers mentioned advantages. In many ways the advantages were the obverse of the problems, as one teacher wrote:

> Advantage: we start from scratch.
> Problem: we start from scratch.

Those who talked about the advantages concentrated on the lack of tradition in a new town and on the *freshness* of the children. One teacher thought that the pupils at the school were more energetic and enthusiastic but also much cheekier than he had encountered elsewhere.

Some teachers said that being attached to a new school with a pioneering function was a most rewarding task for them; that is, it provides them with much hard work and associated prospects of promotion. As we can see, however, all the so-called advantages were in a sense negative ones, and boiled down to the lack of any opposing school traditions in the area. The vast majority of answers tended to concentrate upon the difficulties inherent in working in a community uprooted from the slums of a large city. One teacher, who was by no means a middle class academic type, summed it up:

> The problem is the lack of any kind of intellectual tradition, abetted by a solid proletarian community being rehoused intact, untouched by a more aware class of people. There is almost no real middle class presence in the town, no feeling of gentility, few old people. A paucity of experience is available. TV, pubs, beat clubs, and dances, commercial radio, fish and chips, betting shops—that almost comprehensively lists all influences outside family, friends and school. Problem: to induce more critical attitudes

especially in relation to mass media. Advantage: no saturated market for anything you can contribute.

It is significant that this teacher was one of those who wished to experiment with the curriculum and to try out new teaching methods away from the class room.

Many of the staff reiterated the difficulties of working in an area where there were, as they said, no books in the houses, no tradition of scholastic work, bad home conditions, children with low I.Q.s and a great deal of thieving and vandalism. Many of the criticisms expressed were directed more against the planning authorities than against the people themselves, however. As we have seen, the town was made up of 60,000 people, rehoused almost overnight, of predominantly young married couples with families, despatched to an area lacking many of the necessary amenities and with little or no sense of community. It was this problem that the teachers saw themselves called upon to tackle, and naturally they felt that they were committed to a kind of social missionary work. As one senior teacher expressed it:

Social and welfare problems abound in Kirkby and there exists an odd attitude among many adults that their misfortunes are none of their doing and that the world owes them a living. *It is one of our tasks to re-educate already indoctrinated youngsters away from this attitude.* . . . To some parents the standards imposed by the school of uniform, behaviour and especially loyalty (other than loyalty to the gang!) are harsh and alien. One feels acutely at times that some of the pupils live between two culture patterns— the essentially 'middle class' tradition of hard work, respectable dress, good conduct, etc., presented by the school, and the worst elements of 'working class' ideals, including antipathy to everything appertaining to 'them', disregard for property, authority, etc. Fortunately, this comes into the open only with a minority of our parents/pupils, but one feels it may be more widespread among an apathetic majority.

Here we get an insight into the attitude of mind of many

of the teachers who realise that they truly represent an alien culture in a largely indifferent community. Many of them emphasised the fault of the parents, the conflict between 'Them' and 'Us' and the lack of responsibility; as one put it, 'we've got to get through to the children in spite of the parents'.

To be fair we must emphasise that there were some teachers who felt that it was not the fault of the parents so much as their lack of opportunity, and who emphasised that the school should try to bring together the best of working class and middle class values.

Whether this difficulty of conflicting values between school and neighbourhood can best be resolved by a paternal 'we must do them good' or by a more democratic 'we must help them' approach is not the issue. The important point is that nearly all the teachers felt that a clash of values existed. Most, by no means all, blamed the parents; many unashamedly wished to impose middle class values on the children, despite their parents. A teacher who was very sympathetic to the problems of the neighbourhood and very critical of traditional grammar schools ('which turn out maladjusted competent children who are half educated') reported that one of his pupils was a newspaper boy who, out of 120 daily newspapers, delivered '58 *Express*, 42 *Mirrors* and the rest *Sketch* etc.'. He commented that it was the job of the school to change this.

Some go even further and frankly want to change the whole social system which has brought this clash of culture into being in the first place.

## VII

Some of the most interesting comments we have already quoted were obtained by asking a long question about the role of the teacher. The question read as follows:

We would like to have some understanding of what you think the role of a teacher should be in this school. For instance, should the teacher try to inculcate middle-class standards or should he accept the values of the surrounding locality? Please comment on this question with special references to matters of slang, manners, ambition of the children, appearance of the children, etc.

Forty-six of the teachers answered that the teacher's job was simply to raise standards. Twenty-six or about one-third of the respondents, however, most interestingly found the answer more complicated than this. While agreeing that their job was to raise standards, they felt uneasy about the way the question was phrased. Some roundly and jusifiably abused the question. One respondent retorted, 'What do you mean to be middle class standards anyway?' A few tied themselves up into knots in trying to answer the question, as the indignant man who wrote: 'Middle-class standards are rot: and we should not try to encourage children to accept them; we should, however, try to encourage them to be neat and tidy, ambitious and well mannered and try to discourage slovenly appearance and attitudes.'

Perhaps the best summary of the conflicting attitude produced by this question is the following quotation from a young English teacher in the school:

If by middle-class standards you include such qualities as curiosity outside the narrow necessities of domestic survival, an interest in working for or contributing towards a better community, a richer body of interests to absorb your energies, then I suppose the answer must be yes, we are inculcating these values. The alternative possibility contained in your question would, if true, render us superfluous, wouldn't it? Or at best, policemen.

Our question did bring out very clearly the differing values which the teachers had. It showed that a large minority felt a real moral problem faced them as educationalists in a community of this nature. On the other hand the majority saw no problem of conflict and were quite content to bring outside or alien values to bear upon the children.

The first point that this raises is that all the teachers' replies showed, as we have already seen, that they realised a conflict existed between themselves and the community, and even those

who were sensitive to imposing 'middle-class' standards felt
that they certainly had to promote some higher standards.

The second point is that it is extremely interesting to find
out what other attitudes were held by the twenty-six teachers
who realised the conflict and were worried by it. Generally, as
we have seen, these teachers were senior in the school's hierarchy. Their reaction was probably due not so much to
seniority as such as to the policy of appointing senior teachers
who were sympathetic to the problems of the community. Fifty
per cent of the senior teachers as opposed to 25 per cent of the
junior gave answers which indicated that they were aware
of *and* worried by the conflict of values. Teachers with degrees
were no more likely to give such 'conflict conscious' answers
than those without, but teachers of Arts subjects were more
critically aware of this difficulty, over 50 per cent giving a
'conflict conscious' answer as opposed to 32 per cent of the
whole group. Significantly more of the 'conflict conscious'
respondents were, as we would expect, favourable to experiments with non-streaming, less in favour of caning, and were
on the whole less critical of the pupils' parents than those who
saw their job as simply to raise standards. There was no
significant relationship with age.

Thus the overall impression is that a third of the teachers,
especially those in senior positions, were actively aware of both
the moral and the social difficulties implicit in their role. On
the whole they tended to take what is called the 'progressive'
line on all scholastic questions. They were also much more
committed to thorough going change and social reform than
the majority who tended to be critical of the community and
who wished only to raise its standards. The latter also took
a more conservative line on other questions.

It is perhaps paradoxical that those teachers who most
wished to change the social situation were on the whole more
aware of the conflict which naturally arose between the values
of school and the values of the community, and most troubled
by it. The majority who merely wished to inculcate middle-
class standards were not in a personal way nearly so committed
to the people living in the school area as were the reforming

minority. In fact their attitude to teaching was based on the more traditional grammar school approach which sees education mainly as a possession of the middle classes and as a means of social mobility for the more gifted members of lower income groups.

In a society which is moving in the direction of real secondary education for all it is the teachers who realise the clash of values in all its fulness who seem to be more committed to social change. They understand, however, that schools in this kind of community will have to effect a successful compromise between the values of the neighbourhood itself and the traditional values of middle-class education if they are to achieve their intentions and ambitions.

To conclude, therefore, it is only possible to understand this school and the teachers in it by using a modified conflict model. There are in fact three different patterns of conflict. These are:

1. between progressive teachers and the mainly middle-class standards of society;
2. between progressive teachers and the mainly working-class standards of the local community;
3. between conservative teachers and some of the working-class standards of the local community.

There is no conflict, of course, between conservative teachers and middle-class standards of conventional society.

The future pattern of education, especially in areas such as the town we studied, will be determined by the way in which these three conflicts are ultimately resolved.

# 6

# *Parents and Children*

Although the great majority of Ruffwood pupils lived in Kirkby, a small proportion at the time of our enquiry came from outside the estate. These were children whose parents had chosen Ruffwood as the secondary school they wished their child to attend. Nearly all were from the area of Knowsley Maypole Junior School, which is nearer to Ruffwood than to any other secondary school. The school's policy was that they were accepted as long as this did not exclude children living nearer. County policy has subsequently altered and now the school recruits entirely from its immediate catchment area. It seems likely that the loss of such children is an impoverishment of the school, since the presence of a number of pupils whose parents have deliberately chosen to send their children to the school must be a boost to the morale of the staff and of the other pupils who had no choice.

All fifteen children from outside Kirkby who are included in the survey had failed to obtain grammar school places in the eleven-plus examination. In their socio-economic background, one quarter of, their parents fall in the Registrar-General's Social Class groups I and II, compared with one-fortieth of Kirkby children's parents. It may well be that these parents have chosen Ruffwood because they are anxious to give their children the opportunity of a more academic education than is available in a secondary modern school. None of these parents was among the group dissatisfied with the school.

Table 6.1 compares a number of characteristics in these children and children living on the estate.[1] It would appear that they have a tendency to be more 'aspirant' than their companions and may be assumed to have benefited from their choice of comprehensive rather than secondary modern school.

In the analysis of the survey results, both groups have been included where questions directly relating to the school are concerned. Where questions of location are involved, however, responses from non-Kirkby pupils and parents have not been used.

The analysis showed that the answers to some questions were not informative or reliable enough to be of any value, and these were excluded. For example, a question put to the pupils 'Can you tell us why you want to stay on or leave school?' produced answers for those staying on which were basically 'to get more education' or 'to get a better job', and if leaving, 'dislike of school' or 'to get a job quickly'. In neither case was it felt to be realistic to draw a line between the alternative replies. Similarly, the question to the parent 'Is ......... staying on into the 5th form?' was not used because it was decided that more reliable information could be obtained from the school.

The remainder of this chapter gives an account of the results directly relating to the attitude of pupils and parents towards the school and its policies and the opportunities it provides. Those which concern out of school activities will be considered in a later chapter.

*The extra year*

The pupil's assessment of the value of a year at school additional to that legally required, and of taking G.C.E., must inevitably be a reflection of the value given to these in the school and, to a lesser extent, in the home. The parents themselves may well be greatly influenced by the school through the medium of the parent-teacher association and by the advice given by teachers to the child himself.

Even without the evidence of the teachers, it would be

[1] See Appendix F.

possible to deduce from the responses of the children that at Ruffwood the pressure on the child to remain for an extra year is strong. Fifty-eight per cent of the pupils said that they wanted to stay on, and, even among those who wanted to leave, only four said that they had been told at school that an extra year was not worthwhile for them. Difference in response between boys and girls was negligible.[1]

It would appear that this appreciation of the extra year at school is closely related to a belief in its utilitarian value, for 59 per cent of all children in the survey thought that it was likely to lead to a higher income after leaving school, and 66 per cent that it would help them to get the particular jobs they had in mind. There was naturally a very strong relationship between those hoping to stay on and those holding these opinions: over three-quarters of those wishing to stay on believed that it would improve their financial prospects, and all except five that it would help them to obtain the job they wanted.

Miller's[2] investigation into the attitude of boys at secondary modern, comprehensive and secondary grammar schools also indicates that the practical value of the extra year is important to the child. Given a simple choice between school and starting work, approximately two-thirds of the grammar and comprehensive and five-sixths of the secondary modern pupils would choose to leave. When the extra year is linked to the opportunity of taking G.C.E., the proportion wanting to leave decreased considerably, and around 90 per cent of grammar and comprehensive and 80 per cent of secondary modern pupils in these circumstances would choose to stay.

Comparable attitudes were also found by Blair Hood[3] in a survey of children in their last year at secondary modern schools. Again the proportion of children who would prefer to leave school was a little over three-quarters, with a slightly

[1] Records show that in the event 45 per cent of the boys and 39 per cent of the girls from the 4th form moved into the 5th form in 1965.
[2] T. W. A. Miller *Values in The Comprehensive School*, University of Birmingham Institute of Education Monographs, No. 5, Oliver & Boyd, 1961.
[3] H. Blair Hood 'Occupational Preferences of Secondary Modern School Leavers', *Educational Review*, 1 : 1951.

larger proportion wanting vocational training if they stayed an additional year.

It would be expected in these circumstances that significantly more children in the upper sets would be ready to stay on, for they are likely to be more confident of their ability to succeed in G.C.E. or similar examinations. Only three children in Sets 1 and 2 did not expect an extra year to help them with the particular jobs they wanted, while 86 per cent of these sets believed it would enable them to earn more. On the other hand 55 per cent in Sets 4 and 5 did not expect it to help them in obtaining their chosen jobs, and 40 per cent thought that it would not affect their income.

The social class of the parent was also closely related to the wish to stay on, significantly more with parents in Social Classes I, II and III than in Classes IV and V hoping to stay. Those with parents in Social Classes IV and. V were almost equally divided between wanting to stay and to leave. It would be difficult to decide which of these influences were primary and which secondary, for clearly social class of parent, child's set, and his estimated value of additional education are all closely interrelated.

The proportion of Ruffwood parents who wished their child to stay at school was slightly higher than that of children who wished to do so: a reflection no doubt of their confidence in the education being provided. There was, however, a tendency for those mothers who were not working to want their child to leave. Only two fathers and three mothers whose child wished to stay on would have preferred him to leave, but there were twenty-six fathers and the same number of mothers whose child wanted to leave but who would have preferred him to stay. Related to this about 70 per cent of both husbands and wives believed that the extra year would help their child in obtaining employment, although significantly fewer wives who were not working appeared to believe this. There was also a relationship with the social class of the father here, significantly more in Social Class I, II or III wishing their child to stay on.

There seems little doubt that the influence of the teacher has been important in producing this result, for all of those whose child wished to stay on and who were aware of the teacher's opinion said that the teacher was in favour of the child's remaining. In nearly three-quarters of the survey families either the husband or the wife had visited the school at some time during the previous year and it is probable that it was at such meetings that the teachers' recommendation of the extra year was most effective, for significantly more of those who had made such a visit wished the child to stay.

## The chosen occupation

In deciding whether to remain at school or not it would seem that it is the teacher whose influence is predominant. In choosing the particular job that they hope to obtain on leaving, however, there is little suggestion by the children that the teacher plays a direct part. When asked whose influence was dominant here, the highest proportion, 40 per cent, claimed that they made up their own minds. Slightly fewer, 33 per cent, gave their parents as their main influence, while an additional 15 per cent combined the two. The teacher, either alone or in combination, was mentioned by ten pupils only. It is interesting here that significantly more children in sets 1 and 2 than in other sets say that they make up their own minds. No differences in attitude were evident between boys and girls.

Advice on careers is given mainly in years four, five, and six. Third year pupils would be offered very general guidance but would not meet the Youth Employment Officer.

It would seem that the teachers are more concerned with the general thesis that an extension of school time will be valuable and in fact it would hardly be practicable to discuss with each individual child the particular employment he might take: nevertheless 15 per cent of the children said that they had been given such advice.

The job given by the child as the one he wished to obtain has been classified into the Registrar-General's Social Class groups. These are shown in Table 6.2[1] for boys and girls separately and compared in Table 6.3[1] with the occupation of

[1] Appendix F.

their parents. Sex differences are evident chiefly between the manual and non-manual grades: few boys choose the latter and few girls the former. This is almost certainly related to the availability of suitable jobs and reflects the differences in structure between male and female employment. There are too few choosing professional occupations to be sure that the predominance of boys here has any significance, and there is certainly no difference between the sexes when Social Classes I and II are taken together. All five girls who opted for occupations in Social Class V specified 'factory work' and may be presumed to be unconcerned with the nature of the work they take, while the single boy in this group, opting for 'van boy' had probably also given little thought to the question.

Comparing the wished-for occupations of the children with that of their parents, both boys and girls showed highly significant differences[1] in an 'upward' direction: the numerical description accorded to the social class groups is accepted at its face value.

Parents, when asked what job their child wanted to go in for and to say what they would prefer if they disagreed with this, overwhelmingly supported the child's choice. Eight per cent of those who did not, were more aspirant than the child and 5 per cent were less.

The choice of occupation made by secondary modern school children in Ealing in 1948 (Wilson)[2] and in North-West Lancashire in 1949-50 (Jahoda)[3] is included in Table 6.2 for comparison. Comparison should strictly speaking be made with Ruffwood's Sets 3 to 5 only. Table 6.4, which gives occupation by set, may be used in conjunction here. There is an obvious shift towards occupations in the higher social class groups by the Ruffwood children. None of the Ealing boys or girls and only one boy from North-West Lancashire chose professional occupations, while a far from negligibile proportion in each survey chose unskilled manual occupations. Wilson

---

[1] Non-parametric 'sign' test.
[2] M. Wilson 'Vocational preferences of secondary modern school-children', *British Journal of Educational Psychology*, xxiii, 1953.
[3] G. Jahoda 'Aspirations in secondary modern school leavers', *British Journal of Psychology*, xliv, 1953.

and Jahoda both compared the I.Q. of the child with that which they considered was required for the jobs and both obtained a very low (though significant) correlation of 0.3. Wilson comments that the most intelligent boys chose clerical work or the Forces, it may be assumed because these gave some hope of improvement to the more ambitious child. He states that fewer than 5 per cent chose occupations 'unsuited to their educational standing as pupils of a secondary modern school'. Blair[1] also reported a 'realistic attitude' taken by nearly 300 children in secondary modern schools, where the great majority chose skilled or semi-skilled occupations, but only four boys and twelve girls mentioned occupations in Social Classes I or II. Jahoda found a tendency for sons of semi-skilled or unskilled workers to wish to enter skilled occupations, but sons of skilled workers were content with that level.

Table 6.4[2] gives a broad grouping of occupation chosen by the set the child belongs to, and bears out the 'realistic attitude' mentioned by Blair. Nearly half of those hoping for occupations in Social Classes I or II are from Set 1, significantly more than from other sets, and none are from Set 5. Three-quarters of the manual and two-thirds of the non-manual occupations which need some skill are chosen by children in Sets 3 or 4, while five out of the six children choosing unskilled work are in Set 4 or 5. It may be noted that half the children uncertain of the job they want are in Set 4, where there might be some difficulty in knowing what is within their capabilities.

While significantly more children hoping to obtain jobs in Social Class I or II than others believe that the extra year at school will help them to earn more money, of the remainder nearly half of those wanting manual work and one-quarter wanting non-manual are unsure how much difference it will make. The first is probably related to the continuing preference of employers for taking boys into apprenticeships at the age of fifteen years, while in few trades is a reduction in the length of apprenticeship allowed to the boy who has stayed longer at school.

[1] *Op. cit.*
[2] Appendix F.

Asked if they wished to become an apprentice or train for a job in some way after leaving school, 58 per cent replied that they did. Significantly more of these were boys, reflecting their bias towards manual skilled work. A secretarial course, which includes classes in shorthand and typing, may be taken at school, so that for those interested in this type of work little further training would be necessary.

More than 90 per cent of the husbands and wives whose sons had taken part in the survey were in favour of either apprenticeship or other training for them after leaving school. The approval for qualifications of some sort is therefore overwhelming. Taking into account that one-third of the fathers were unskilled or semi-skilled manual workers, that is without formal training, this would indicate little belief in a future for this type of worker in spite of the relatively high wages available at the time of the survey.

## Parents' attitude to education

It appears that the attitude towards additional time at school on the part of the parents is relatively both informed and progressive, and some indication has been noted that school policy has been transmitted either directly from the teachers or indirectly through the pupils or both. The first part of this chapter has been specific to the child. More general attitudes were also investigated. For example, parents with children of both sexes were asked whether they believed that schooling is as important for girls as for boys. There was no significant difference in response between husbands and wives, two-thirds of whom agreed that it is.

All parents were asked whether they agreed with the compulsory raising of the school leaving age to sixteen years. Slightly fewer parents agreed to this than said that they thought an extra year would help their own son or daughter to obtain a job, but they were nevertheless a high proportion: about two-thirds. There was a slight but significant difference between the attitudes of husband and wife here, wives being less able to give a definite answer. Significantly more husbands in Social Classes I, II or III were in favour than others, but this did not apply to wives.

Over 80 per cent of both husbands and wives said that they were in favour of comprehensive education, as opposed to a grammar/secondary modern system, and about 90 per cent were satisfied with the education provided at Ruffwood. The approval is unambiguous, for more than 80 per cent of husbands and wives separately declared that they wished that they themselves had been able to spend additional time at a school like Ruffwood. Approval of comprehensive education is most probably a reflection of this approval for the school, for few parents were likely to have the experience or the information necessary to assess relative merits of the two different systems. Less than 10 per cent of the parents had attended other than elementary schools, and no doubt the majority of these were in city areas where standards of construction at least were low. It would be surprising in these circumstances if there was not approval, but perhaps it should not be too easily extended into anything wider.

Dissatisfaction with Ruffwood School, expressed by fourteen husbands and eleven wives, and with comprehensive education generally, were not as clearly linked as might be expected, for half the dissatisfied husbands and nearly two-thirds of the dissatisfied wives still favoured it. The most frequent criticism from these parents was that discipline is poor. This was closely followed by the opinion that the school is too large to allow individual attention to pupils, and, by the husbands, that it is poor academically, not enough homework being provided or too much sport. It may well be relevant that five out of ten sons of dissatisfied parents were described by them as backward, and there had been difficulty in controlling two out of ten daughters.

## Attitude to Kirkby

It would seem evident, from the attitudes of parents and children considered in the previous sections towards vocational training and the type of employment hoped for, that there is a widespread desire among the children to improve upon the economic or social position held by their parents. It is relevant, in these circumstances, to discover whether parents wanted their children to remain in Kirkby when they were grown up, and whether children for their part thought they would want to do so.

Only about one-third of both husbands and wives had distinct views on this question, the remainder responding 'Don't mind', 'It's up to them', or 'Don't know'. Those who gave a definite response were almost equally divided between wanting their child to stay or to go (Table 6.5[1]). There was no evident divergence between the husbands and wives in their views, but among the husbands significantly more in Social Classes I, II and III wanted their child to leave than those in Social Classes IV and V.

These responses probably reflect more a compliant basically 'working-class' attitude with regard to their children's wishes, and a belief that this is a matter for them to decide, than any lack of interest in their whereabouts when they are adult.

Among the children, more definite views were given, although it must be borne in mind that these are more likely to be an indication of attitudes related to ambition and aspiration than evidence of what will in fact occur when the time arrives. Nearly half the children said that they thought they would want to move out of Kirkby when they were older, while another one-third were unsure. The remaining 16 per cent alone believed that they would want to stay (Table 6.5[1]).

No significant differences were evident between boys and girls, but significantly fewer of those hoping for jobs in Social Classes I and II than in other groups expected to remain. This may be a by-product of the relatively small number of jobs of this nature available within the town, or of the fact that the number of people in professional or managerial occupations living in Kirkby at the present moment is negligible, so that there is an association between holding these positions and living outside the town. This is an aspect of Kirkby life which many who are responsible for its future hope to eliminate, and

[1] Appendix F.

is a problem that is frequently encountered in a community of this type.

As the more aspirant children tend to belong to Sets 1 and 2, it might be expected that the same association is found for children in these sets compared with those in Sets 3, 4 and 5 as for those looking for occupations in Social Classes I and II.

Comparing the attitude of parents in this respect with that of their children, it is interesting that no association was found between either the father or the mother who wishes their child to leave Kirkby, and the child who believes that he will. On the other hand, significantly more of those children who expect that they will want to stay in Kirkby have fathers who also want them to stay. This relationship does not arise between mothers and their children. It may be that a positive encouragement to remain may influence the child more strongly than one which implies an acceptance of his disappearance from the family circle, from however worthy a motive, or of his having to make the final decision.

## School uniform

At Ruffwood children wear school uniform, in the words of the Head, 'to encourage loyalty to the school and to establish the status of the school in the neighbourhood and beyond'. In this country, uniform is generally associated with the grammar and public schools and it is possible that its frequently praised characteristics relating to conformity, tidiness and suitability for school activities are now of less importance than the standards of education which it implies. In the struggle to build up a tradition and a respect for the quality of education equal to that which is usually accorded without question to the grammar school, it may be argued that uniform can have a not inconsiderable effect. However, to the working-class parent, these advantages may well be less compelling than the expense which it entails.

Answers to the question whether parents are in favour of school uniform were among the few in which there was a significant divergence between husband and wife (Table 6.6). Although very few were uncompromisingly against uniform,

TABLE 6.6. PARENTS' ATTITUDE TO SCHOOL UNIFORM

| Attitude to Uniform | Husband | | Wife | |
|---|---|---|---|---|
| | Number | Percentage | Number | Per cent |
| In favour | 122 | 67 | 177 | 83 |
| Against | 16 | 9 | 4 | 2 |
| In favour but for cost | 42 | 23 | 28 | 13 |
| No opinion | 3 | 1 | 4 | 2 |
| Not present at interview | 34 | Excluded | 4 | Excluded |
| Total | 217 | 100 | 217 | 100 |

proportionately nearly twice as many husbands as wives felt the cost to be enough of a disadvantage to prevent them from showing wholehearted support. It must be assumed that in Kirkby this is a household expense which is borne mainly by fathers. Nevertheless, the figures show that the principle of school uniform is accepted: further evidence in fact of the parents' confidence in the policy of the school.

## Homework

Homework may be compared with school uniform to the extent of being, at least until recent years, mainly associated with a grammar school education. It is generally believed to be essential to a course designed to advance pupils to G.C.E. standard and may therefore have similar status-conferring benefits.

About a third of the pupils in the survey stated that their homework took them more than half an hour daily and, as might be expected, Sets 1 and 2 spend a significantly longer time over it than others. An equal number admitted to spending between a quarter and half an hour, while the remainder either did less than this or none at all.

Only 5 per cent of the husbands and wives interviewed were not in favour of their son or daughter having to do homework, although there was the occasional qualification 'as long as there's not too much'. There was a negligible amount of uncertainty on this topic: only three parents were unsure. It would be interesting to know whether a similar response would have been obtained during the first years of Ruffwood's existence. Considering the difficulty there must be to provide conditions suitable or even possible for homework to be done, this nearly unanimous approval is surprising.

An attempt was made to discover where in fact homework was done, and whether any coercion by the parents was necessary. However, it was decided that the answers were too unreliable to use, few parents being ready to admit that TV and homework might run concurrently or that their child was other than willing.

## Sex instruction

A very high proportion of parents were in favour of sex instruction in the school (Table 6.7),[1] although many emphasised that it should supplement instruction given by the parents. At the meeting with parents when the staff explain their efforts in this direction they emphasise very strongly their desire to help parents in *their task* rather than suggesting that they are trying to take over the parental role. A significant difference between husbands and wives was evident in the responses, more husbands than wives approving. This is traditionally a woman's concern, at least when she has a daughter, and the divergence is not perhaps as unexpected as the high proportion of mothers who did agree to the school's taking over their role in this respect.

## Discipline in the school

It has already been noted that the most frequent criticism of Ruffwood mentioned · by dissatisfied parents was that the discipline there is 'poor'.

The majority of Ruffwood parents certainly appeared to have few qualms about the use of physical punishment in the school, even for girls (Table 6.8). Well over half the wives and nearly three-quarters of the husbands believed that teachers should use a cane on both boys and girls, while a relatively small proportion, which however included significantly more

Appendix F.

TABLE 6.8. PARENTS' ATTITUDE TO USE OF THE CANE

| Use of cane | Husband | | Wife | |
| --- | --- | --- | --- | --- |
| | Number | Percentage | Number | Per cent |
| Agree for boys | 32 | 18 | 38 | 18 |
| Agree for boys and girls | 134 | 73 | 127 | 60 |
| Disagree | 13 | 7 | 39 | 18 |
| Don't know, not certain | 4 | 2 | 9 | 4 |
| Not present at interview | 34 | Excluded | 4 | Excluded |
| Total | 217 | 100 | 217 | 100 |

wives than husbands, disapproved of caning entirely. There was nevertheless a significant difference between the attitude of husbands and wives where caning girls was concerned, relatively fewer wives than husbands approving of this.

Caning at Ruffwood is generally discouraged and kept as a final resort; it is then used only with the knowledge of the parents. However, teachers in the school vary considerably in their personal opinions as to the use and value of corporal punishment.

## Discipline in the home

Asked for their opinions on disciplining adolescents generally, nearly half the parents emphasised their own responsibility, while another quarter believed that the school had an important part to play in addition to themselves. There was a tendency for the belief in a divided responsibility to be more often held by parents in Social class groups I, II, and III than those in IV and V. Only 7 per cent of all parents believed that the responsibility was the school's alone.

Various shades of opinion were revealed in the parents' comments, ranging from: 'Not a clue! No way to stop them' to 'Things are all right as they are.'

A number mentioned the different relationship between child and teacher at Ruffwood from that prevailing in their own school days, some apparently feeling that this had led to a lack of respect for the teacher which diminished his capacity to apply disciplinary action. For example, comments were:

'Teachers seem more friends than teachers—they're not

scared of them'; and (disapprovingly) 'They're allowed to talk to teachers any way they like.'

It was generally acknowledged that the father should be the ultimate power in the home, and the problem for those mothers whose husbands were on shift work and so rarely saw the children was mentioned. Working mothers were frequently blamed for lack of discipline—by non-working mothers—and it was suggested that in many homes parents were out working all day and in clubs or pubs all night. Attitudes which might indicate this type of behaviour were certainly not evident from the comments received, however. The great majority of parents seemed genuinely concerned, if not troubled, by the problem of discipline and there was little attempt made to minimise their own responsibility. The comment: 'If there's any trouble, it's up to the Probation Officer' was unique.

## Vandalism

Kirkby has become well known in the Merseyside area for the destructive activities of its young people. Telephone kiosks are smashed as soon as repaired, and similar acts of destruction committed in the district are unusually high. Parents and children were both asked what they thought about the gangs alleged to be responsible for vandalism in Kirkby. The replies cut across social class groups. Nearly a third of all parents made the comment, either alone or in combination, that the stories had been exaggerated. 'The Press puts them in the limelight', and 'It's not just Kirkby' were typical remarks.

About half the parents felt that stricter measures of one sort or another were required, and 18 per cent of all parents believed that birching would be a remedy. This was an entirely unprompted suggestion. A stronger police force and stricter measures by the police were suggested by many. On the other hand, some parents pointed out that a good deal more could be done by the general public, who are apparently often afraid to intervene when they see a gang at work.

A number pointed out that gangs are not necessarily

malicious; for example, 'Some gangs do good work; one gang is bad and the rest are branded', and 'Gangs perhaps cling together for support but this is not much different to being organised later on into Trade Unions.'

A quarter of the parents believed that a good deal could be done to improve the situation by providing more facilities and entertainments for teenagers. 'Sport's the finest thing for curing high spirits' and 'Big Business should spend money on playing fields' were two comments, countered by another: 'Vandalism is probably by youths of a type who would not go to entertainments even if they were provided.'

A few suggested that overcrowding, especially in flats, was the trouble; for example: 'Too many kids in this area—it's a losing battle,' but many hoped that it would improve in time. In the words of one father: 'We must hope that civic pride and community spirit will develop, but the town hasn't settled down yet.'

Responses from the children to the same question ran along very similar lines to those from their parents, with no differences evident between those of the boys and girls. About half made comments showing disapproval of vandalism which were variations on one boy's succinct response: 'I think they are nut cases.'

The opinion that stories about the gangs are exaggerated was held by significantly more children whose parents made similar comments, but other reactions did not appear to be related in this way. Typical comments in this group, which contained 17 per cent of the children, were:

'I've seen these gangs, in fact I've been in one and they don't go around with steel chains. We are very board [sic].'
'Some papers make a mountain out of a molehill and so the gangs try to live up to their name.'
'Some of the gangs are quite nice people.'

One or two of the children said that they had been attacked by gangs and also that individual members away from the gangs were often afraid of other boys. More entertainment and facilities of various kinds were suggested by 16 per cent, one of whom commented: 'This is done by a small minority of provokated adolescents. There's nothing to do so they bust a few windows for fun.'

Admitted approval of vandalism was negligible, and perhaps the attitude of some of the more thoughtful is summed up by one girl who said: 'Some of it is true but three-quarters of it's lies. They just try to give us a bad name. Every new town has its disadvantages.'

In the circumstances it is not surprising that a great many of the children (75 per cent) said that if they saw someone breaking into Ruffwood school, they would report it to the police.

# 7

# *Teachers and Parents*

In Chapter Six the ambitions or expectations of parents and children for the after school years were considered from their own personal point of view. Responses by teachers to questions bearing on this subject are of particular interest. These questions which are mainly from Part IV of the teachers' questionnaire (see Appendix B) were 'directed primarily towards those who have a responsibility for the placing of children in their future occupations'. In the event only forty-five of the eighty-one teachers taking part in the survey completed any questions in this section, and few of these answered all of them. This limited response must be borne in mind when considering the opinions expressed.

Asked in general terms whether the aim of Ruffwood was to send their late leavers to technical or training college rather than to universities, three points of view were put forward by equal numbers of respondents to this question, totalling thirty-six in all. One third expressed unqualified agreement; a further third qualified it with comments to the effect that, though this was not a direct aim, it would occur, or that, while it occurs now, it is less likely to do so as time goes on. Disagreement was shown by the remaining third who emphasised that the child must be encouraged to obtain the most suitable training according to his or her abilities.

Surprisingly few teachers appeared to feel that they had the necessary knowledge to deal with the question of what particular problems face children living in Kirkby when they look for jobs. Most certainly felt that the school's connections with local industry could be closer and that there should be a great deal more cooperation in both directions. Talks by industrial personnel officers to the pupils and visits to firms were both recommended. It was also suggested that more information from firms as to what they required from their employees might be supplied and that the firms themselves would also benefit from consulting the school when considering engaging its former pupils. Some criticism was also made of the Youth Employment Service, mainly to the effect that the number of officers was inadequate for the work required and the suggestion was made that the school might provide its own Youth Employment Officer.

The few teachers answering questions on employment problems for Ruffwood pupils mainly believed that able children should find little difficulty in obtaining jobs, but that this might well involve leaving Kirkby where too few appointments for trained people, especially girls, are available at the present time. A number of teachers commented that there is an unwillingness on the part of parents to encourage this, and that some children, particularly girls, are reluctant to leave home. On the other hand, about as many considered that as far as apprenticeships go there are not enough capable people in Kirkby at present to take the work that is available on the Trading Estate, and that local jobs should as a matter of policy be filled by local people.

These rather divergent opinions may be reconciled by applying the first to the college or university trained Kirkby resident and the second to the skilled manual or non-manual worker. Firms on the Trading Estate in fact need at present to look for many of their skilled workers in districts outside Kirkby. The high proportion of semi-skilled and unskilled manual workers resident in Kirkby as compared with Liverpool has already been discussed in Chapter Two.[1] At the same time, there has been to date little demand for the highly qualified, and, in particular, the University trained, man or woman. A photographic research establishment which is to be opened

[1] The Town of Kirkby.

shortly will require a number of physicists and chemists: this is an entirely new venture for Kirkby, and it is hoped that success in recruiting suitable staff here will encourage others of a comparable type.

The apparent impression which teachers have of a lack of ambition among parents for their children or again (a frequently occurring comment) too great a tendency to leave the decision on a career to the whims of the child can only be judged against the responses of parents which bear on this question. It is certainly evident that nearly all parents supported their child's choice of occupation. On the other hand the choices made by the children would seem both realistic and, as compared with their parents' occupations, generally aspirant. With regard to leaving Kirkby, most children hoping for professional occupations appear to realise that this will involve leaving the town, and nearly half of all pupils in the survey in fact expect or hope to leave when they are older. Parents, reasonably enough, are less wholehearted about this, but only 17 per cent specifically stated that they wished their child to remain.

This apparent divergence between teachers' impressions of parents' attitudes and the attitudes displayed by parents' responses is again evident in teachers' answers to the question 'Do you find parents interested in the work of the school?' This was answered by the full complement of eighty-one respondents, sixty-three per cent of whom criticised parents in some way while only three per cent generally approved of them. The remainder expressed no definite opinion. Yet parents' attitudes, at least as far as could be judged from answers given in the survey, did not appear to be lacking in interest and certainly showed little opposition to the aims of the school, educationally at least.

In deciding whether the parents' expressed opinions should be accepted or not without qualification, it should of course be remembered that the questions were put to them by young undergraduates, whose opinions on further education and related subjects could be inferred, even if they were not expressed. There may well have been some hesitancy on the part of many parents to put forward opinions to their interviewers which they knew would meet with even unexpressed disapproval.

Teachers' opinions of the parents appear unrelated to seniority, age, type of subject taught, political inclinations, or support for comprehensive as opposed to bilateral education. However, two sets of opinions do appear to be related significantly. In the first, in answer to Question 15 (see Appendix B) relating to the role of the teacher: whether to inculcate 'middle class' standards or to accept the values of the surrounding locality, significantly fewer of those who believe there is some value in local standards are positively critical of the parents. The second, a less positive piece of evidence, is that all seven of those who were generally approving of the parents find Ruffwood children, by and large, cooperative.

Many teachers who were generally critical of parents were nevertheless ready to give credit to a small group in F.R.S.A.[1] who work hard and actively. Its fund-raising capacity was often mentioned although at times it was commented that this appeared to be almost its sole function. Some teachers also appeared to think that in spite of this hard working minority the association would collapse but for the help of the staff.

Teachers' criticisms of parents were rarely that they were positively antagonistic or interfering, but rather that they lacked interest and were apathetic. A suggested breakdown by one respondent was: 20 per cent devoted supporters, 30 per cent passive supporters, 30 per cent indifferent and 20 per cent hostile. Another commented: 'The society as a whole does not believe in contact with school—this is a "middle class" concept.'

It appeared that most teachers felt that parents should play a positive role at least where the future of the child was concerned. Two-thirds of those answering the question as to whether school, parent or child should make the choice regarding a pupil's future course or career replied that all three were concerned. None suggested the school alone, or the parent alone, but a number stressed that the child should make

[1] The School's Parent Teacher Association.

the final decision, while a few explained their belief that the parent should not be involved by suggesting that they tended to be 'financially minded'.

Most teachers obviously feel that they are involved in a struggle to open out opportunities for their pupils of which they might in other circumstances and in other places be unaware. If the results of Douglas's[1] investigations are generally applicable, it can be accepted that children of parents in manual occupations, particularly where these are unskilled, even when they have high ability have particular difficulty in reaching an educational standard equivalent to that of their peers of 'middle-class' background. Douglas[1] has demonstrated that the level of interest shown by parents in their children's education, as measured by the number of their visits to school in a year, can be related to the child's achievement at the eleven-plus examination. This is not necessarily a direct cause and effect relationship, but it can be understood that with this in mind, teachers are discouraged by an apparent lack of interest which the rarity of the voluntary visits by parents appears to show. On the other hand, it is very possible that Kirkby parents generally do not yet understand that such visits are expected or even that these can provide any help to the child which the teacher is not equally or more capable of supplying himself. It would certainly appear that in a number of directions, such as a belief in the value of education continuing beyond compulsory limits, and an acceptance of standards of dress and behaviour set up by the school, the school has in fact made a considerable impact on parents, which must imply a positive interest on their part. It is very possible that this is a situation which will improve in time as mutual understanding and sympathy grow between the parents and teachers.

[1] J. W. B. Douglas *The Home and The School*, MacGibbon & Kee, 1964.

# 8

# *Leisure*

The development of the Kirkby township followed a similar pattern of construction to that found in most of the housing estates throughout the country: a concentration on house building for some years at the expense of all but the most fundamental community facilities. Only gradually was provision made for the organised recreation of young Kirkby residents outside the home. In the meantime, a tradition of vandalism and other petty lawbreaking had inevitably developed among the town's teenagers. No doubt many factors were involved besides a lack of recreational facilities, some inescapable, such as a decrease in parental control as a result of parents' absorption in a move requiring considerable social and psychological adjustments. A longer journey to work for many fathers, resulting in less time spent at home, may also have contributed. This particular point will not be pursued here; it has been studied and reported in detail in many other localities. In a previous chapter, the attitudes of parents and pupils towards anti-social conduct has been given and discussed. It shows little overt sympathy and a perhaps wishful belief that reports have been exaggerated.

In this chapter some account is given of the leisure activities of Ruffwood's fourteen year old pupils at the time of the survey, which must be considered against a background of the recreative facilities that are generally available in Kirkby. Facilities for young people in the town have been gradually built up, the first steps being taken by voluntary organisations associated with the churches and schools. One of the earliest youth clubs, Centre 63, built and maintained by the Church of England, is now grant aided and has a full time leader and permanent accommodation of its own. This is the largest of the Kirkby youth clubs, with a membership of 650 and an average nightly attendance of 150. In addition there are six maintained youth centres with part-time leaders, four based on schools and the remaining two on temporary and rather makeshift accommodation. These have nightly attendances of between 50 and 100.

On an individually smaller scale are four youth clubs run by churches on an entirely voluntary basis and organisations such as Scouts, Guides, Church Lads Brigade, Girls Friendly Society, Junior British Red Cross and Air Training Corps. The Scout and Guide troops together have a combined membership of about 600. An evening institute caters mainly for the educational interest of fifteen to twenty year olds, while in 1964, Kirkby Urban District Council provided a sports stadium with a gymnasium, racing and cycle tracks and an athletic arena.

There would therefore appear to be a fair range of activities open to young people in Kirkby, and the number of clubs and other societies available to them must now compare favourably with the provision made in most larger towns and cities. Yet when that has been said it remains a fact that the total number of boys and girls on the estate between the ages of fourteen and nineteen years is approaching the 9,000 mark, and it is unlikely that more than 2,000 can be covered by the recreational facilities available.

It is, of course, true that many who are not members of gangs or social misfits simply do not choose to make use of the town's clubs and societies. It may well be that today an increase in the number of youth clubs of the type at present in existence would attract few members as yet unattached elsewhere. Involvement varies considerably with age, and at fourteen years, the age of our Ruffwood survey children, there is likely to be less interest in some forms of activity such as dancing or field and track athletics than there may be two or three years later. Few clubs in fact cater for this age group at all, although the Ruffwood school club is a shining exception to this rule.

Our enquiry was concerned with frequency of attendance at a number of social and other activities, but in considering the results, it should be borne in mind that we are speaking only of the fourteen year olds and findings for these cannot be extended to include children who are either older or younger.

Both Kirkby and non-Kirkby residents have been included in this section of the survey, but responses in the two groups have been compared throughout, and any differences have been noted in the text. Inclusion was thought to be justified because this part of the report is concerned with the usual recreational interests of fourteen year olds, living at some distance from a city. This applies to both groups equally.

The pupils were asked how often they went to a cinema, dancing, the 'Cavern' or similar 'beat' club, to the school club or any other youth club. The answers could be given in one of four categories, ranging from 'never or rarely' to 'more than once a week', with the exception of the school club. This meets only once a week for any one age group and the fourth category was, therefore, omitted and 'occasionally' substituted for the second.

TABLE 8.1. ATTENDANCES AT THE CINEMA, BEAT CLUB, SCHOOL CLUB, YOUTH CLUBS AND DANCING

| Attend: | Number | Per cent |
|---|---|---|
| None | 40 | 19 |
| One out of five | 63 | 29 |
| Two out of five | 44 | 20 |
| Three out of five | 48 | 22 |
| Four out of five | 19 | 9 |
| All five | 3 | 1 |
| Total | 217 | 100 |

Out of the 217 survey pupils, only three, all girls, take part in all five activities with a greater frequency than 'rarely', while forty (19 per cent) claimed that they never or rarely attend any of the five. Of these forty, thirty-two were boys and eight were girls.

More than a quarter of the children attend only one of the five more often than 'rarely'. For nearly half these children it is the cinema which is visited and, for most of the remainder, it is the school club. Frequencies of attendance at all five types of entertainment are given in Table 8.1 and individually in Table 8.2.

TABLE 8.2. FREQUENCY OF ATTENDANCE AT THE SCHOOL CLUB, CINEMA, DANCE HALL, YOUTH CLUBS AND BEAT CLUB

| | Frequency of Attendance: | | | | | | Total Responding | |
| | Never | | Less than once a week | | Once a week or more | | | |
| | No. | Per cent | No. | Per cent | No. | Per cent | No. | Per cent |
| --- | --- | --- | --- | --- | --- | --- | --- | --- |
| School Club | 105 | 50 | 74 | 33 | 38 | 17[1] | 217 | 100 |
| Cinema | 122 | 58 | 80 | 35 | 14 | 7 | 216 | 100 |
| Dance Hall | 139 | 64 | 44 | 20 | 32 | 16 | 215 | 100 |
| Youth Clubs (other than School Club) | 159 | 73 | 22 | 10 | 36 | 16 | 217 | 100 |
| 'Cavern' or similar Beat Club | 170 | 78 | 31 | 14 | 15 | 8 | 216 | 100 |

N.B. Non-responses have been excluded.

Overall frequencies did not differ between Kirkby and non-Kirkby residents, but attendance at youth clubs did vary significantly. Children living outside the estate are less likely to attend the school club and more likely to attend other youth clubs. This is almost certainly related to the distance of their homes from the school: an evening journey back to Ruffwood probably seems not worthwhile when other youth clubs are nearer at hand.

The school youth club meets once a week during term time and is the best attended of the entertainments enquired about. Even so, half those interviewed said that they never attend it. Another third attend only occasionally and the remaining 17 per cent weekly. Attendance was not found to be related to the child's set.

The cinema is the second best attended entertainment, with a little over a third of the children saying that they go regularly, though less than once a week, and 7 per cent once

[1] Frequency of once a week.

a week. As Kirkby has no cinema of its own, such a visit usually means travelling into Liverpool and so must be a relatively expensive outing with fares on top of admission fees. More than half the children apparently never go, possibly for this reason. Provision of a cinema headed the list of amenities which parents suggest are needed in Kirkby and was a very close second on the children's list. It can be assumed that the proportions of cinema goers would be substantially changed if a local cinema was available. (This seems unlikely at present as the cinema proprietors do not believe that the population is large enough to support one.)

Significantly more children from Set 1 than from other sets go to the cinema at least occasionally. Forty-two per cent in Set 1 said that they never go compared with 67 per cent in Sets 2 and 3 and 51 per cent in Sets 4 and 5.

Youth clubs in the town and beat clubs, which again usually require a trip to Liverpool, are patronised to a similar extent. About three-quarters of the children do not go to either, but 16 per cent go to a youth club and 8 per cent to a beat club once a week or more. Significantly more in Sets 1, 2 and 3 than in Sets 4 and 5 go at some time to a beat club.

Dancing takes up an intermediate position with a little more than a third of the children going at least occasionally. Again this must generally mean travelling to Liverpool.

It would appear that girls of the age interviewed are more likely to take part in these social activities than boys. Significantly more girls than boys attend either all or all but one of the five considered here. In particular, significantly more boys than girls said that they never go to a beat club, the school club or dancing. Only the cinema and town youth clubs are as likely to be attended by boys as by girls.

This tendency towards a greater social participation on the part of girls extends also to church going. A third of the survey pupils said that they attend a church, chapel, lodge or Sunday School at least once a month and these included significantly more girls than boys. There are few Roman Catholics in the school, so that it is probable that the proportion of church attenders in Kirkby generally would be higher.

An attempt was made to discover whether the survey children usually spend their leisure time with one friend or in a group, but it was felt that a reliable answer to this question required more than the superficial enquiry which was all that was practicable in this case. In answer to the question 'Who do you spend most of your leisure time with?' two-thirds gave 'a group of friends' as their answer and a little more than a quarter mentioned a single friend. The remaining 5 per cent said that they spend most of their time either alone or with members of their family.

The boys and girls were asked as a separate question whether they had a steady girl friend or boy friend respectively, though it was not considered that the answers should be taken too seriously, or too literally. A quarter replied that they had, among whom there was a tendency towards more girls than boys. No significant differences were evident here between sets. As would be expected considering the age of those asked, about half of these friends were older and half about the same age. Girls were more likely to have boy friends older than themselves and boys to have girl friends of about the same age—only very occasionally were they younger.

It has been remarked that a number of leisure activities considered here probably involve a journey to Liverpool. The 1960 survey of Kirkby has shown that for older members of the family, the great majority of whom have lived in Liverpool for most of their lives, ties with the city remain strong. Visits to relatives and friends and shopping excursions are comparatively frequent. Nearly half the Ruffwood survey parents, both husbands and wives, said that they go to Liverpool, other than for their jobs, once a week or more and nearly two-thirds go at least once a month. There was no significant difference between Kirkby and non-Kirkby residents here, nor in the frequency of visits made by husbands and wives, but when asked for their reasons, shopping and visiting relatives were both mentioned in about 40 per cent of Kirkby wives' responses, and in 22 per cent and 30 per cent respectively of their husband's. These two activities together were given by the non-Kirkby parents in very similar proportions, but here shopping was mentioned rather more often than relatives. Other reasons for visiting Liverpool were much less frequently given (Table 8.3).

TABLE 8.3.   REASONS FOR VISITING LIVERPOOL

| Reasons for Visits to Liverpool | Husbands | | Wives | | Pupils | |
|---|---|---|---|---|---|---|
| | Number | Per cent | Number | Per cent | Number | Per cent |
| To Visit Relatives | 73 | 35 | 103 | 45 | 139 | 24 |
| Shopping | 54 | 26 | 97 | 42 | 122 | 22 |
| To Visit Friends | 20 | 10 | 15 | 6 | Not asked | |
| Football Match | 25 | 12 | – | – | 61 | 11 |
| Cinema | 9 | 4 | 7 | 3 | 83 | 15 |
| Pub | 21 | 10 | 4 | 2 | Not asked | |
| Dancing | Not asked | | Not asked | | 14 | 2 |
| Clubs | Not asked | | Not asked | | 14 | 2 |
| 'Messing about' | Not asked | | Not asked | | 85 | 15 |
| Other | 5 | 3 | 4 | 2 | 51 | 9 |
| No response or not interviewed | 34 | excluded | 4 | excluded | – | – |
| Total reasons | 207 | 100 | 230 | 100 | 569 | 100 |

N.B.   More than one reason was allowed.

Asked how often they visit Liverpool, most pupils and their parents said once a week or more. A third of the survey pupils said they went once a week and another 19 per cent more than once. Of those remaining, about half said that they go to the City once a fortnight and half once a month (Table 8.4). There

TABLE 8.4.   FREQUENCY OF PUPILS' VISITS TO LIVERPOOL

| Frequency of Visits | Number | Per cent |
|---|---|---|
| Never | 1 | – |
| Once a fortnight or less | 100 | 46 |
| Once a week | 77 | 35 |
| More than once a week | 39 | 19 |
| Total | 217 | 100 |

was no significant difference here between Kirkby and non-Kirkby residents. Among those making the journey most often, boys appeared to be involved as often as girls, but of those going less often, significantly more boys than girls go only once a month or less.

Most children gave two or more reasons for visiting Liverpool, and as might be expected, seeing relatives and shopping were mentioned most frequently by the Kirkby residents, each contributing to about a quarter of their total responses. For non-residents, a visit to the cinema replaced the relatives. These three activities together with 'messing-about' accounted for three-quarters of the responses in both groups. It was hoped that this latter category might cover the generally motiveless wandering among the shops which may fill in an empty afternoon or evening. Eleven per cent of the visits were to attend a football match, and any remaining activities such as dancing and clubs were a small proportion of the whole (see Table 8.3). Among the occasional activities, watching or taking a trip on the ferry boats which cross the Mersey from Liverpool's Pier Head, and going to the swimming baths, occurred most often.

Only two home based leisure occupations were enquired into: watching television and reading. All except 10 per cent of the pupils admitted to watching television at least some of the time and 40 per cent replied that they watched it 'a lot'. There was no obvious overall relationship between watching often and interest in entertainment outside the house. On the other hand, significantly more boys than girls said that they watched television 'a lot' and this agrees with our finding for their lesser involvement in outside activities.

Significantly more pupils from Sets 1 and 2 said that they watched television only 'a little' than those in other sets. Eighteen per cent in these two sets replied that they watch little, compared with 11 per cent in Set 3 and 5 per cent in Sets 4 and 5. There was an associated tendency for those hoping for non-manual occupations to watch television less often than others.

It was thought that the reliability of answers to the question on what books, papers or magazines had been read outside school recently, depending as it largely did on memory, was questionable, but that a simple distinction might be made between those who gave the name of at least one book and those who mentioned only magazines. On this basis, slightly more than half fell into the first category and slightly fewer into the second. About the same proportion said that they do or do not use the public library, confirming the division into 'serious' and 'non-serious' readers in broad terms.

Differences in the responses of boys and girls to the questions relating both to type of reading and use of the library were not significant. On the other hand, significantly more pupils from Sets 1 and 2 use the library, the percentages declining from 64 per cent in Sets 1 and 2 to 39 per cent in Sets 4 and 5. A similar gradient was evident in the proportions of 'serious' readers, dropping from 71 per cent in Sets 1 and 2 to 24 per cent in Sets 4 and 5 (Table 8.5). Associated significant differences between those hoping for manual or for non-manual jobs

TABLE 8.5.  PUPILS' BOOK READING AND USE OF LIBRARY BY SET AND HOPED FOR OCCUPATION GROUP

|  | Sets 1 and 2 | | Set 3 | | Sets 4 and 5 | | Hoped for occupation groups[1] | | | |
|  | | | | | | | Non-manual | | Manual | |
|  | No. | % | No. | % | No. | % | No. | % | No. | % |
|---|---|---|---|---|---|---|---|---|---|---|
| Readers of Books | 47 | 71 | 25 | 45 | 23 | 24 | 50 | 59 | 28 | 33 |
| Non readers of Books | 19 | 29 | 25 | 45 | 71 | 74 | 33 | 39 | 55 | 65 |
| No response | – | – | 5 | 10 | 2 | 2 | 2 | 2 | 2 | 2 |
| Total | 66 | 100 | 55 | 100 | 96 | 100 | 85 | 100 | 85 | 100 |
| Users of Library | 42 | 64 | 29 | 54 | 37 | 39 | 57 | 67 | 33 | 39 |
| Non users of Library | 23 | 35 | 25 | 45 | 59 | 61 | 26 | 31 | 52 | 61 |
| No response | 1 | 1 | 1 | 1 | – | – | 2 | 2 | – | – |
| Total | 66 | 100 | 55 | 100 | 96 | 100 | 85 | 100 | 85 | 100 |

were similar. Books were mentioned by 75 per cent of boys and girls hoping for jobs in Social Classes I and II, 49 per cent of those wanting non-manual jobs in Social Classes III and IV and 33 per cent of those wanting manual jobs. A comparable pattern was shown in the use of the library (see Table 8.5).

Parents' answers to the question, 'What do you enjoy reading?' were combined and again reduced to a simple division between families where at least one parent reads books of some kind and those where only papers or magazines were

[1] Only those giving an occupation have been included.

mentioned. Proportions were very similar to those given by their children, about half appearing as 'serious' and half as non-serious' readers. This is obviously a crude distinction and also weighs against those households where only one parent was interviewed. Surprisingly, there was apparently no relationship between parents and children who are 'serious' readers, though this may be due to the crudeness of the categories, or to unreliability in the answers. That this is so is indicated by their being little more than a tendency towards a gradient between 'serious' parent readers in Social Classes I, II and III, and those in Classes IV and V, when highly significant differences might have been expected.

Only about 10 per cent of both husbands and wives feel that there is enough for young people to do in Kirkby and when asked specifically about youth clubs, 70 per cent of both thought there should be more. Parents and pupils were asked to make suggestions as to what is needed for young people in Kirkby. These, broadly grouped, are given in Table 8.6.[1] The agreement between the two on the need for a cinema has already been mentioned. Swimming baths, a cinema, and facilities for sport of some kind were the three most frequently mentioned suggestions in both lists. Probably youth clubs figured less often than they would have done a few years ago, and the frequency with which they were mentioned in this context does not suggest that there is any feeling of urgency that their numbers should be increased in spite of the high proportion previously mentioned as stating that there should be more. A dance hall seemed a greater need to the parents than to the pupils, but it is likely that there would be more agreement on this with older children.

It would appear that those who are concerned with the well being of young people in Kirkby are well aware of the deficiencies in the town, and a great deal of effort is being spent in making them good. School swimming baths are now available at times outside school hours to members of youth organisations, and a Sports Centre is being built as well as a large youth centre and additional youth clubs.

[1] Appendix F.

A report by Lancashire's Chief Education Officer estimates that in 1965 over three-quarters of the young people in Kirkby were unattached to any of the organisations provided. Provision for the eleven to fifteen year age group is particularly needed since within this age group are those juveniles most open to the risk of committing offences. Without a cinema, dance hall, bowling alley or coffee bar in the town, yet with a ratio of teenagers to adults as high as or higher than that in any New Town in the country, Kirkby poses a tremendous challenge to official and voluntary organisations alike. In the struggle to channel adolescent energies into socially acceptable activities, the influence of the school is fundamental. That Ruffwood appears to accept such a responsibility seems evident from comments made by the teachers. To quote from two of many similar responses:

The need in Kirkby is to nurture a community spirit and thence an awareness of civic responsibility in children whose background has not previously contained any such elements. A great disadvantage is the 'rootlessness' of a new town. And: . . . such qualities as a curiosity outside the narrow necessities of domestic survival, an interest in working for or contributing towards a better community, a richer body of interests to absorb energies: . . . We are inculcating these values.

# 9

# *Summary and Discussion*

## *I*

Ruffwood, it will be clear, is not representative of all comprehensive schools. In so far as it is a new building in a new residential area it has been able to avoid some of the difficulties which have beset comprehensive schools in some parts of the country. Not only was there no well-established grammar school in the locality to compete with, but the vast majority of the residents had little or no firsthand experience of more advanced forms of secondary education. This probably meant an absence of initial prejudice against the school. At the same time, however, the very lack of family contact with more academic institutions must have made the work of the school accordingly more uphill.

There are therefore advantages and disadvantages associated with the pioneering of comprehensive education in what is virtually a new town such as Kirkby. We cannot say whether the advantages outweigh the disadvantages or vice versa. We do know, however, that the task facing the school was and still is a formidable one. Whether the school be seen as primarily concerned with changing the culture of the immediate community or whether it is thought to involve a much more thoroughgoing social mission, there is no denying the special problems that the staff had to face in a new township like Kirkby. The development, as we have already seen, was unusually rapid, involving the migration of many thousands of people in the space of less than ten years. The new residents had in the main been living previously in overcrowded and

104

physically blighted inner residential districts in Liverpool. Their pattern of living hence was inevitably more adapted to the tightly-knit community life of the older city neighbourhoods than to the much more open and unfamiliar features of the new town layout. The families, moreover, tended to be large and to contain a great many young children. Kirkby is also, of course, a one class town. The population was and still is overwhelmingly working class, the majority of those employed being in manual occupations of varying degrees of skill but with an unusually high proportion of unskilled workers. Many of the Kirkby women go out to work and no less than half the mothers of pupils at Ruffwood were found to be employed at the time of the survey.

As we have already seen, Ruffwood occupies a spacious site and was purpose built. Equipment and facilities in the main are of a high standard although at the present time facilities for sixth formers are extremely inadequate. The main problems that the school had to face arose on the one hand from the nature of the pupils' social background, and from the size and complexity of the school itself on the other. It has always had to face a stiff task at the purely academic level. So serious indeed was the question of the pupils' ability in the early days that doubts were expressed regarding the possibility of the school being able to arrange adequate fifth and sixth form work. In spite of the presence of many children of apparently low I.Q., the history of the school's development has shown that these original fears were largely groundless. Staff of high academic standard have been attracted. The proportions of pupils staying on after the statutory leaving age have steadily increased over the years. By September 1966 there were 248 pupils in the fifth year: 54 per cent of the age group. Sixty-three, or 16 per cent of the age group, were in the sixth and forty-four in the Upper Sixth or, to put it in another way, in their seventh year of secondary education, forming 11 per cent of the age group. Between September 1965 and September 1966 the sixth form had grown from 80 to 117 pupils. Examination results also indicate a steadily improving performance over the years. The seventh annual report of the

Headmaster makes a number of significant points on this topic and we will quote from it verbatim.

On the subject of the so-called 'Newsom Pupils', he has this to say:

An encouraging number of pupils of average or less than average ability choose to remain at Ruffwood for a fifth year and, though the C.S.E. examination[1] is not in theory designed to provide for any but the most able of these boys and girls, it was thought desirable to enter almost all of them for the examination in at least a few subjects. Only seven of the pupils so entered failed to do sufficiently well to achieve a certificate and it seems probable that the school will continue to enter, at least until the raising of the school leaving age, almost all of its fifth year pupils for an external examination.

On the G.C.E. 'O' Level results the Headmaster reports:

The total number of subjects passes in the summer of 1966 was 399, as compared with 243 in 1965 and 200 in 1964. Though both the number of candidates and the age group from which they were drawn were larger than previously, it is clear that the 1966 results represented a very considerable improvement on previous years.

1966 was the first year in which a substantial number of Ruffwood pupils were of the normal age to take the 'A' level examination, and twenty-four pupils had some success, sixteen of them obtaining two or more passes, providing a minimum university entrance qualification. Some of the grades were high and the results in general were better than had been anticipated.

Seven pupils, all boys, secured admission to universities, nine (five boys and four girls) to colleges of education, and these will almost certainly be joined by five others (three boys and two girls) in 1967.

[1] The Certificate of Secondary Education was instituted by the Minister of Education on the advice of the Secondary Schools Examination Council following the report of the Beloe Committee, and pupils first took it in 1965. The idea was that an external test somewhat below the standard of G.C.E. 'O' level was desirable for the average and slightly above average secondary school population as an index of their ability and effort and also as a possible guide to prospective employers.

The Headmaster then makes a most interesting further comment at this point:

> It is worthy of note that one university entrant and five of those going to colleges of education entered the school with transfer scores from primary schools suggesting that they were of below average intelligence and ability and that only three of the sixteen who had gone on to post 'A' level further education could possibly have been given Lancashire grammar school places at eleven years of age.
>
> More recent figures relating to the 1961 intake show that thirty (approximately 7%) went on to enter higher education, eighteen of whom were reading for degree courses.

We think that the evidence of these figures suggests not only that the school has made quite remarkable academic progress during the first seven years of its existence, but that, furthermore, it is succeeding in saving talents which might otherwise have been lost and in giving late developers a chance to retrieve their unpromising start. Morale, amongst both teachers and pupils, is important in any school and increasing levels of achievement in any and every sphere of the school's life will tend to improve subsequent performance as confidence is gradually created within the group. In this way, it can be seen that a school like Ruffwood is at one and the same time helping to meet an unsatisfied demand for more education on the part of the local community and also stimulating even greater demands in the same direction.

As one possible way of making some comparative assessment of the school's achievements we considered trying to imagine what might have happened to these pupils had they still been living in inner Liverpool and attending the Crown Street type of schools. This was a difficult undertaking as Crown Street has altered during the eight or so years that have followed the first enquiry. The population has fallen, some new residential accommodation has been erected and at least one of the original schools has been replaced by a modern building. Furthermore, selective secondary provision has expanded in the city as a whole during the intervening period and some comprehensive schools have come into being. Conversations with officers of the local Education Authority suggested that the ex-pupils of Crown Street schools today secure more selective places than they did a decade ago, although accurate figures were not available. One of the researchers, however, did visit three central area Junior schools and found that while a substantial improvement in the situation was reported in one area, where extensive redevelopment had occurred, in the others, as far as could be seen, things had not greatly changed since the publication of *Education and the Urban Child*. Our evidence here is largely impressionistic, however, and must be regarded with caution. Even if there are signs of improvement in the Crown Street area there is no reason to believe that, contrasted with suburban schools, its schools are not still greatly disadvantaged and under-privileged. We think, although we are not in a position to prove, that the children of the families who have been rehoused in Kirkby and who have attended such schools as Ruffwood have thereby been able to make more educational progress than they would have done if they had remained in the old neighbourhood.

While we would not want to assess the school's success merely in terms of improving academic performance we quote the examination figures given above as offering perhaps one comparatively objective indication of the school's achievements in an important aspect of its life. There are a number of other probably equally vital areas and here again the evidence is impressive. We found, for instance, that no less than 90 per cent of the parents interviewed expressed unequivocal support for Ruffwood School, even though a small minority of them had some reservations about the idea of comprehensive education as such. There was very strong support indeed for the wearing of a school uniform. Sex instruction in school was also very favourably received and there was near unanimity on the value of homework being set. Indeed, an interesting and slightly discrepant finding of our enquiry amongst the teachers themselves suggests that they tended to underestimate the degree of support that they were receiving from the home. This may arise because of their own professional modesty; it may also arise partly from the fact that parental support is

not always expressed very actively by attendance at scho
functions. We have to remember in this connection, howeve
that working class culture is traditionally rather estranged
from school life, that most manual workers tend to think of
themselves as being somewhat inferior vis-à-vis the teaching
profession, and, that furthermore, in their own school days
the parents had not known many teachers who encouraged
active cooperation between school and home.

We think that the evidence derived from our enquiries
shows that the parents of Ruffwood pupils are well disposed
towards the school and that, as time goes by and as the teaching
staff make increasing efforts to break through the traditional
barriers separating school from neighbourhood, a much more
positive attitude will develop and cooperation between parents
and teachers will become accordingly much stronger. We
would emphasise, however, the temporal and cultural lag
which is clearly still operating in the Kirkby situation and
stress the fact that it is the teachers with their greater sophisti-
cation and expertise on whom the major responsibility for
establishing links between school and neighbourhood, teachers
and parents, depends.

One additional fact which suggests that the school is having
a real impact on the locality is the comparative success of the
school clubs. Here we can see the beginning of a process which
could produce richer and richer dividends of goodwill and
collaboration as the years go by. Associated with this is one of
the criticisms made by many parents that the teachers are too
friendly with the children and that discipline (as judged by
memories of their own schooldays) is slack. Here again we find
evidence of temporal and cultural lag which only the hard
work and determination of the teaching staff will ultimately
make good. As we shall argue later, teachers' professional
attitudes are the key to the solution of this as of most of the
other problems that the school faces.

## II

A second group of problems is associated with the structure
and size of the school itself. Critics of comprehensive education
often put this forward as one of their main objections and it is

clearly a matter of considerable educational moment. Most authorities with experience in the fields of education or child care insist on the need for every child to have the opportunity to belong to a small face to face group with whose affairs he can identify himself and in which he can find some significant role to play. We would not want to deny the validity of this viewpoint. We would, however, query the assumption that often lies behind objections to large schools as such, that is, that the head teacher is unable to know each pupil individually, and that this is a fundamental weakness. We would argue that on the empirical level it may not matter which member of the teaching staff has a personal relationship with a pupil so long as every pupil enjoys such a relationship. At a large boarding school, for example, it may well be that the headmaster knows only the sixth form in any intimate way, but so long as the housemaster and his wife are doing their job properly the pupil is not likely to be neglected or his personal needs overlooked. In a school of the size of Ruffwood it is obvious that it is not part of the ethos that the head should know every pupil. The vertical system with its divisions into eight separate houses and their smaller tutorial groups has been designed precisely to reproduce in a large day school some of the advantages of the conventional boarding school. And our evidence on this point seems unequivocal. Only nine of the eighty-one teachers who responded to our questionnaire considered that pupils lacked adequate contact with members of the teaching staff. Furthermore, our data indicated that the housemasters were the first people to whom a majority of the pupils said they would turn to for support and guidance. The teaching staff were warm in their approval of housemasters in general and of the house system itself.

It was against the paper-work (often thought to be excessive) that most members of staff inveighed. Some of this administration was an outcome of the school's size and complexity. Much of it is probably necessary and unavoidable. As one teacher commented, 'It's too complex but could a better system be devised?' It seems to us that this is another illustration of time-lag, in this case on the part of the educational authorities themselves in failing to appreciate that the organisation of a large comprehensive school is different in kind from that which is deemed to be appropriate for the smaller and compacter school with which most of the administration will be familiar from their own experience.

The fact that it is impossible to run a large scale institution as though it were a small scale one is a truism that is sometimes overlooked. As one of our respondents put it:

> It is not generally accepted that one of the advantages of a very big school is that it becomes an economic proposition to provide first-class ancillary services, for example, a really competent bursar, a nurse, and a welfare officer under school control, a superintendent of buildings (instead of a caretaker), ancillaries at the disposal of heads of departments, and possibly a student-parent counsellor on the American pattern.

It would be tempting to add, admittedly from a financially irresponsible position, a qualified librarian and secretarial help for other senior staff as well as for heads of department. The main point we would wish to make, however, is that since a large scale institution necessitates a division of labour with a view to greater efficiency, this argument might very sensibly be applied to all aspects of the school's life and to all categories of staff. It might be useful to leave this more in the form of a question than as a direct suggestion for policy: would not all-round efficiency be much improved by making additional appointments of the sort suggested above than, in a time of teacher shortage, striving to improve the present staff-pupil ratio?[1]

Should the foregoing question be answered affirmatively by the authorities we would be in a better position to see that in some respects not only can the alleged disadvantages of size be overcome, but that numbers in some respects are a positive advantage. In addition to the more varied syllabus that a larger and more variously qualified staff make possible there are some expensive items of equipment; for example, a swimming bath,

[1] Which stands, at the moment, at about 1/18.

which become feasible only when large numbers of children have to be served. Once it is realised that there are viable ways of overcoming the difficulties of teacher-pupil relationships and similar organisational problems, some of the rational arguments against large scale schools are answered. We do not wish to become involved, as a result of this enquiry, in the party political issues raised by the comprehensive school idea and we would not want readers to deduce from what we have said that a policy of conversion to the comprehensive system is the appropriate solution in every case and in every place. We would say, however, that, on the basis of the evidence which we possess, for this one school in the North West the problems presented by size and large numbers are far from being insoluble or necessarily disadvantageous.

## III

At the same time, it would be foolish to deny that some very real difficulties remain. Some of these arise from the structure of a big institution as such and some seem to be much more subtly connected with individual personalities and attitudes.

During the course of our enquiry we became particularly interested in the question of the 'role set' of the teacher in a school of the magnitude of Ruffwood.[1] In Chapter Three we discussed our analysis at some length and we tried to delineate the way in which the structure of the school led inevitably to a differentiation of roles on the part of the teaching staff. This seems to us to be a subject of considerable importance and we would like to refer to it again as it was obviously a matter of deep concern to many members of the staff. Broadly speaking, the distinction in teaching roles lay between those whose responsibility was primarily for the teaching of a subject (the heads of department) and those whose job was primarily social and disciplinary (the housemasters). We found that the latter

[1] Role set is a technical sociological term which implies understanding that an individual in a social system has many different kinds of relationships in his job with other people. For example, a teacher as teacher has relationships with pupils, parents, other colleagues, the local inspectors, etc., all of which involve different attitudes and expectations.

were almost uniformly popular and acceptable while the former seemed to create occasional feelings of hostility amongst some of their colleagues. The existence of a special heads of departments' common room highlighted this situation. The closing of this 'bastion of privilege', as some called it, during the course of our research possibly went some way to removing this criticism.

We must, of course, point out that this differentiation of roles occurs mainly in respect of special responsibilities. The bulk of the staff are both subject teachers within a department and house tutors. Housemasters are also, for most of the day, subject teachers under the control of a head of department. Similarly, a head of department, unless left out of the tutorial system because of some particular administrative responsibility, will also be a house tutor under the control of a housemaster. The difference, where it is not solely attributable to a clash of personalities, arises from different degrees of emphasis occasioned by an individual's primary and secondary pedagogic functions. This is something which may be inevitable in the organisation of a large school where a variety of tasks have to be carried out by the same members of staff. In order to overcome serious differences of outlook it would seem to be necessary for both subject heads and housemasters to become aware of the complexities of their roles so that they may be enabled to guard against mutual misunderstanding.

At the structural level a greater degree of communication between all levels of staff would be helpful and more particularly between subject heads and housemasters. At the level of personal attitudes (some might even call them ideologies) an effort might be made, possibly by informal group discussion, in the direction of attaining a more general agreement about the function of a secondary school and the associated role of the teacher in a community such as Kirkby. It seems apparent that heads of departments and other teachers with strong interests in academic subjects, who themselves have been educated and trained to teach in a selective system, are being asked by the nature of this particular school to adapt their work to a philosophy of education which may be somewhat foreign to them. Conversely those members of staff who feel themselves impelled to work towards social amelioration and who have a missionary purpose may at times consider that the demands and attitudes of the more subject-oriented colleagues are defeating their own goals. But at Ruffwood, because of the fact that the social environment is culturally homogeneous and solidly working class, the school finds itself obliged to work at times against some of the local norms. This produces feelings of conflict and perhaps of guilt in the minds of those members of staff who are most personally committed to the school's social function. They may also feel themselves frustrated by certain formal aspects of the school's organisation. This may lead them to be very critical of the school's administration not because they are hostile to its aims but because they are identified with them, rather as patriots are sometimes found in the ranks of the most severe critics of their own countries.

The reformist minded teachers seem to be striving to raise the norms of the surrounding culture and, at the same time, trying to preserve all that is best in the traditions of the local people. They tend to be well disposed towards them, very sympathetic and non-critical. At the same time they want to bring them into line with the main cultural stream of contemporary British society. They want them to have the training and advantages of education that the middle classes have traditionally enjoyed but they don't want them to lose their working class loyalties and solidarities as a result of greater opportunity. On the other hand the more traditional type of teachers want to bring their pupils into the middle class culture because it seems to them the best way of life they know. They are therefore fairly critical of the norms of the surrounding community and want to improve standards but are not so concerned with wider ideas about equality and social justice which motivate their reformist colleagues.

It is very clear that a school which, like Ruffwood, has a reforming purpose tends to attract and to hold those teachers who are most in sympathy with its socially reformist aims while those less in sympathy feel themselves obliged to restrict their commitments to subject teaching and moral training. Or they get out. Any understanding of what is taking place in the school, then, demands attention being paid to the attitudes of individuals both to school work and to the kind of society in which they believe. A study of values becomes essential to an analysis of the school as a functioning institution. We can see how individual teachers are attracted to the social mission implicit in the ethos and aim of such a school and how this identification with its goals serves to reinforce this overriding purpose. Hence we are led to question the idea that a school merely serves to reflect the existing social structure or that it inevitably must by and large reinforce the status quo. It can aim at producing social changes of a specific kind and it can do this, moreover, while engaging in a degree of conflict with the local subculture, aiming, as it were, to create a new consensus, to produce a synthesis of reform and moral agreement on a fresh level of mutual understanding on either side, that is to say between school and neighbourhood, teachers and local families. Here the comparative homogeneity of the community both helps and hinders the process of change— the old urban working class traditions being on the whole indifferent to educational aspirations but, at the political level, committed to supporting a national party which has adopted the comprehensive school as an instrument of social justice and ultimate reform.

At the risk of some oversimplification, then, we can postulate two different kinds of teachers: those stressing academic achievement as opposed to those stressing social welfare, or to put it another way, those emphasising the instrumental and those emphasising the more expressive aspects of their role. The difference is in the main between those who see education as exerting a specific or a more diffused influence.

We think that both aspects of the teacher's role, the 'instrumental' and the 'expressive', are vital to the successful operation of a school such as the one we have studied. Recruitment should not be exclusively geared to the performance of the school's social and ideological function. Academic work must always be an important part of the life of any good school and hence the academic level and scholastic commitment of many members of the teaching staff should be of the highest obtainable. Obviously the ideal type of teacher for a comprehensive school in a socially homogeneous new town such as Kirkby would be the man or woman who combines scholarship with strong reformist zeal. At sixth form level, moreover, it is probable that a teacher's actual teaching skill and his dedication to his own academic specialism will exert a very special appeal to boys and girls who may be going on to higher education. It seems that the more socially oriented work of the housemasters will be most usefully applied to the lower forms. If this is the case, there are grounds for making the sixth forms fairly distinct from the remainder of the school. At the moment, as we have said, accommodation for them is inadequate, and future policy, if suitable physical provision can be made, might well lie in the direction of the creation of a more autonomous sixth form group more in line with the ethos of the separate sixth form college or the college of further education.

However that may be, we think that we can now see, as a result of our enquiry, much more clearly the nature of the important social adventure that is taking place in Ruffwood and similarly situated schools at the present moment. The school stands at the meeting point of two very distinct scholastic traditions and methods: the more theoretically inclined and intellectually demanding grammar school, on the one hand, and the more socially ameliorative and intellectually less challenging secondary modern, ex-elementary school, on the other. It is precisely in this area that comprehensive education is likely to make its distinctive mark by attempting to bring these two traditions together and producing a third, compromise, situation. Inevitably, as we have argued, this will precipitate a degree of conflict between teacher and environment. Paradoxically, as we have also argued, it is probably those teachers who are most aware of the conflict who will nevertheless be in the vanguard of it. It is these teachers, too, who have the most to offer towards the solution of the general problem of secondary education in places like Kirkby for they are the ones preeminently who are striving to offer this new and compromise kind of educational experience to the children and the families of the neighbourhood we have been studying.

There are three possible outcomes or solutions to problems posed.

1. That the middle class standards come to predominate and that communities like Kirkby in the end come to accept these standards.
2. That the community rejects these middle class standards and, in a sense, rejects the advantages of an extended, more demanding and personally more rewarding education with them.
3. That a compromise is reached between the middle class nature of formal secondary education and the working class values of the local community.

Those who believe in the efficiency of comprehensive schools, in our view, seem to be committed to this third solution and this is the objective that they are aiming to attain. Progressive teachers, hence, will be fighting on two fronts; attempting to change society and at the same time trying to change the local community. It is the outcome of this operation of what may be called a creative conflict which will determine the place and nature of secondary education in predominantly working class districts. Here, in a nutshell, is the contribution that the comprehensive school has to make to the wider question of achieving a pattern of education which, without imposing a narrow uniformity, can meet the varying needs of different individuals equally and fairly as part of a national programme which aims, in Robin Pedley's words, to achieve 'a free, classless, diversified, creative society'.[1]

We think that on balance the evidence we have presented in this report indicates firmly that Ruffwood School has already, in its brief seven years of existence, made important steps in this direction and that, in the future, its contribution will become even greater.

[1] R. Pedley *The Comprehensive School*, Penguin Books, 1963, p. 176.

## IV

A few paragraphs ago we spoke about the special needs of sixth formers in the school and here we would like to make a few comments on what is popularly termed the teenage peer group culture as it affects the life of the area. In Chapter Eight we presented data regarding the leisure activities of the middle school group and we noted that their attendance at the school club, although by no means universal, was encouragingly high. In fact proportionately more attendances were put in at the school club than at any other adolescent group not excepting those offered by commercial organisations. John Eggleston[1] has suggested that it is 'the potential strength of the adolescent community' in predominantly working class neighbourhoods that may, in the final analysis, prove to be crucially important in deciding the success of such a school as Ruffwood. If what he calls 'strategies of coexistence' can be worked out between school and peer group it may well be that comprehensive schools will 'discover new resources in their task of matching the holding power of the selective schools'. The great educational problem at Ruffwood and Kirkby, as in similar localities, is how the average and below average pupils can be so enthused that they improve their scholastic performance and so identify themselves more and more with the aims and objectives of the school at every level of its activities. It may be that enlisting the support of the peer group would go a long way towards the solution of the problem of the residual pupil which heretofore has seemed the most intransigent one that such schools have to face. We would suggest that an extension of the activities of the school club, coupled with an intensification of extracurricular groups, should be seriously considered to this end. A deepening of fellowship between pupil and teacher would very likely pay academic dividends. People are usually more inspired by other people than by ideas. Pupils, it has been noted, often enjoy learning a particular subject if

[1] Environment and Comprehensives', *Education*. 28 January 1966, p. 196.

they like an individual teacher. The greater the degree of psychological identification, therefore, that teachers achieve by sharing the out of school and leisure time activities of their pupils, the more the latter are likely to enter into the scholastic work (which the school must as a school take very seriously indeed) with that degree of enthusiasm that the teaching staff desire.

It was not part of our brief in this enquiry to make suggestions regarding the development of youth service in Kirkby or in the county in general. But the incidental evidence about leisure activities and the obvious existence of the peer group culture led us to believe that, in this kind of district, a closer link between youth service and formal education would be to the advantage of both. We were, in passing, impressed by a further suggestion made to us by one of the housemasters to the effect that the school club should try in the future to train future youth leaders and in this way provide a solid basis for the development of youth work in Kirkby as a whole.

Such are the hopes for the future. And this brings us to our final point. We think we can see at Ruffwood the beginning of what could, in time, turn out to be an example of what has been called a community school—the kind of school in which, to quote Pedley again, 'children, parents, teachers, and others meet and mingle' to create a common institution where 'the fullest preparation for a rich, purposeful life in a democratic society can be gained'.[1] Many positive factors are already present. They need developing further. In addition to the school club and the extracurricular activities, there is the Friends of Ruffwood School Association which might in time develop into an extremely active parent-teacher movement. Former scholars' societies (merely embryonic now in the old boys' soccer team) could usefully grow and expand. But we would wish to see the school open its door to organisations other than those over which it has immediate control. In another publication one of the authors of this report put the case for the community school in a general way which could also be applied to a particular school like Ruffwood.

[1] R. Pedley, *ibid.*, p. 137.

Very briefly I see the community school as the vital focal point for every creative, educational and ethically sound activity and organisation in the surrounding neighbourhood. I see it as the place where leisuretime activities are concentrated, where adult groups are centred, where the local social workers' luncheon club has its meetings, where the visiting probation officer or guidance expert borrows a room. The teacher's role in such a set up is as much that of community facilitator as instructor: the head and the senior staff, above all, having a very special and continuing responsibility for fostering groups and organisations in their area associated with child care, recreation, and support for family and social life.[1]

It would be misleading to suggest that Ruffwood has not got a very long way to go before it can be considered to have come within striking distance of such an objective. But a resolute beginning has been made towards what we can confidently think of as the school of the future. The pattern at Kirkby will differ in many ways from that at Egremont in Cumberland where the Wyndham School is an outstanding example both of the communal theory and of its physical expression. Wyndham, for instance, was initially planned to provide facilities for a futher education centre; its private study accommodation for sixth formers may never become a practical proposition at Ruffwood.[2] But education, we have to remind ourselves, is not solely a matter of buildings and plans and equipment. It is also a way of life and this involves values and attitudes of mind which, to be effective, must be embodied in individual men and women. The final outcome depends primarily on the quality of the staff and above all on the determination and skill of its senior members. Even at the risk of sounding patronising we think that Ruffwood has been well served in this direction but we also think that continuity and stability are important and that these depend upon key

[1] J. B. Mays 'Problems of adolescents: delinquency and the transition from school to work', in *Aspects of Education,* University of Hull Institute of Education No. 5, p. 71.

[2] See a report by G. M. A. Harrison in *Education,* 27 August 1965, for a brief account of the Egremont venture.

members of the teaching staff remaining at their posts for a fair number of years 'to see the job through'.

The first seven years of the school's history have been characterised by numerical growth, development of the curriculum, academic pace-making and standard-setting in the face of considerable social difficulties. This period is now substantially completed. A second phase is now beginning which in its own way will be equally difficult and critical. In this phase consolidation of what has already been achieved will be vital. So, too, will be the need to get even more closely to grips with what Dr Michael Young called 'the task of the century'.[1] By this he means exposing still further numbers of average and below average working class children to 'the influence of education' and thereby releasing them from the cultural bonds which prevent them from realising their full potentialities. This means finding a kind of school that makes sense to them, a school which does not ask them to break faith with their own loyalties and traditions and which, at the same time is in no sense academically second rate. This is, in fact, what Ruffwood has been trying to do with results which so far are encouraging, and the next seven years of its history should see the process brought even closer to fulfilment.

[1] *Innovation and Research in Education*, Routledge & Kegan Paul, 1965, p. 60.

# *Appendix A*

*Examples of Daily Bulletin of Ruffwood School*

## *Daily Bulletin*

Thursday, 7th July, 66.

1. TO ALL STAFF

(*a*) **Rally Committee Meeting** (brief, I hope) in UCB at 4.10 p.m. on FRIDAY, please.

AGENDA: rally preparation plans, briefing, etc. Apologies for 4.10 p.m.! GK.

(*b*) **Sports Day—tonight—7.00 p.m.**

It would help if staff who have volunteered to help could be at the stadium by 6.45 p.m. Track judges should report to HO. Field judges to CA. Other helpers to DO. Dressing room 1 (Boys Side) has been allocated for staff use only. Please come prepared for all weathers. Thank you. DO.

(*c*) **Staff Bowls/Darts Evening—Monday, 11th July.**

Interest and response to this evening has been beyond expectations. However, we are required (by the hotel manager) to limit our patronage/pilgrimage to 50 *persons* (retiring room capacity). Hence, it is necessary to include the first 50 to pay 3/- each to their social rep.

Tickets for the *Valedictory Social* on *Tuesday, 19th July* may be obtained at 5/- each from social reps. RC KH MJ WS JG. Thank you. CR.

(*d*) **Social Reps.** A short meeting in C6 on Friday at 1.15 p.m. (Should Boiler Room be unavailable!) CR.

(*e*) If anyone has a French Doll (any size) which they would be willing to lend for a day, would they please contact Mrs Thomas (DE) during the next few days. HA.

## 2. TO HOUSEMASTERS

(*a*) Meeting in DCR at 1.00 p.m. AGENDA: (1) Rooms, (2) 5th E. and Merit Comp., (3) Girls' Uniform, (4) Office, (5) Form 7Z. IK.

(*b*) Could you please make one final check that all competitors are aware of all instructions for tonight. Could I also have the names of staff i/c teams. DO.

## 3. TUTORS PLEASE ANNOUNCE

(*a*) *S*ports Day—tonight—7.00 p.m.
*Competitors* are reminded that they should be at the stadium by 6.30 p.m.
*Spectators* are warned that they must wear normal school uniform. You will not be allowed in wearing jeans.
*Helpers*—will those boys who volunteered to help meet in B20 at 9.05 a.m. today.                                  DO.

(*b*) Entries for 'Naming the Kids' competition on a piece of paper with your name and house to Mr Inman, Mr Twist or Mr Topping by tomorrow, Friday. IN/TW/TG.

(*c*) P.E. week in the Lake District. All boys going with Mr Carroll and Mr Williams next week, please meet in A19 at 1.15 p.m. on Friday.


## Daily Bulletin

Tuesday, 12th July, 66.

## 1. TO ALL STAFF

(*a*) *Rally* 66. *Briefing Details*
Briefing meetings: —
*Staff in CH* at 3.30 p.m. THURSDAY (P.M. school **ends** after period 7).
*Pupils in CH* at 9.30 a.m. THURSDAY (all i/cs will be required).
*F.R.S.A. in CH* at 7.30 p.m. THURSDAY. GK.

(b) *School Excursions*

   (i) Several excursions recently have been undertaken without the required 3d per head insurance being applied for. May I remind colleagues that ST should be consulted before any excursion takes place so that he may effect the necessary insurance cover?

   (ii) I should be grateful if colleagues taking excursions would kindly let me have, the day before the excursion, the numbers of pupils to be taken from each set or option group. This will enable me to make possible mergers to ease the substitution problem. HW.

(c) The following will be on a visit to a W.R.A.F. station in the Midlands with HT and JL today:—J. Baker 5th; A. Jones and B. Jowett 4th; D. Jones, K. Burleigh, O. Stott, A. Gillies, P. Linforth, S. Ehlen, L. Kelso, 6th. JL.

(d) Any staff arranging working trips to Haydock Park please see JB re transport. JB.

(e) *Senior Club*—would staff who will be coming to club (A and B teams!) kindly let me know if possible. Thanks. RJ.

(f) Would staff who are leaving please return all school keys in their possession to WI in the Tech. Block by tomorrow (Wednesday).

(g) Would any supply teachers who have not handed in Insurance Cards, please do so.

(h) *Part-time teachers.* There is in the office a copy of a memorandum concerning method of payment, terms of notice, etc., which you may care to use.

(i) REMINDERS:—Press Conference 2.30 p.m.; Councillor Tempest talk to 6th form p.m.; 6.00 p.m. First Aid Exam. C7; Tech. Dept. Wood meeting 4.00 p.m.

2. TO HEADS OF DEPARTMENTS

(a) I would be most grateful if H. of Ds. would allow me to have, or borrow, a copy of their 6th Lower Summer Examination sheet, to add marks to College aspirants information sheets. SG.

3. TO HOUSEMASTERS

(*a*) When children are out for the day and do not require meals, we are asked by the School Meals Organiser to inform the Kitchen Supervisor in advance.

4. TUTORS PLEASE ANNOUNCE

(*a*) *Senior Club*—the last club of this season will be held tomorrow. 7.30 to 9.30. Would ALL pupils inform OLD pupils of this. RJ.

(*b*) *V and VI.* Today at 2.50 p.m., Councillor Tempest is to give a talk to ALL pupils in VI form and in English sets V XIX, 10 2N, T1 on the subject 'Regionalism, regional planning and the boundary commission'. HW.

(*c*) *School Council.* There will be a preliminary meeting of the Council on Thursday at 1.00 p.m. in C4. HW.

(*d*) *IV, V and VI.* Rally helpers on admission and programme sales will need a shoulder bag in which to collect cash. GK.

(*e*) *External Exam. Results* (Second Notice) are expected on the following dates: —
*G.C.E.* J.M.B. Advanced and Special papers Monday, 15th August.
Ordinary papers Thursday, 25th August.
A.E.B. Advanced papers Monday, 15th August.
Ordinary papers Monday, 22nd August.
*C.S.E.* The date is given vaguely as 'July'.
*R.S.A.* The date given is 'late August'.
*Pitman.* Results are expected in mid-August.
Note that NO RESULTS will be given by 'phone. The results will be published in the entrance hall of the Administration Block. Any candidate who wishes his/her results to be sent by post must supply the school office with a *stamped, addressed postcard* indicating the results required. DY.

(*f*) There will be a meeting at 9.30 a.m. today in CH for all pupils who have volunteered to sell programmes at the Rally. LL/GA.

(g) *Tennis Tournament*—Singles finals tonight. All pupils taking part should report to GF/GM at 4.00 p.m. today.

(h) *IV, V and VI.* (i) All Careeers Books borrowed from C's should be returned this week at the latest. (ii) Leavers who have not yet secured employment should make a determined effort during the next few days. Pupils who leave it much later may find only 'dead-end' jobs or jobs they are not particularly keen on. The Youth Employment officer is willing to have another chat with pupils (at the Quarry Green offices) on Mondays, Wednesdays and Fridays.

# *Appendix B*

*Ruffwood School Teachers' Questionnaire*

R.T.S.

This questionnaire has been designed to cover all members of staff whether in senior or junior positions or whether they teach science, technical or arts subjects. Consequently it is rather long. We do not intend that you should answer all these questions but only those which are relevant to you or on which you have definite views. If you consider that you have no experience or views on a particular question, please write 'No Comment' in the space provided. Do please, however, answer as many questions as you are able; generally we only expect answers of one or two words or sentences but in cases where you have especial experience, we would value a longer contribution.

## *Part I*

First we wish for information regarding your position in the school and any particulars of previous experience and training. (Please ring or tick alternatives as appropriate.)

1   Ruffwood School Code Letters     Mr/Miss/Mrs     Date

2   Marital Status, M;     S;

3  Position                    Resp. Allowance, Head;  D.H.
                                                        Snr. Mistress

   Part time or Full time      H. of D.        A  B  C  D
                               Grade           I  II  III

   Main Subject                Subsidiary subjects
   Outside activities with pupils
   Other school duties

4  PREVIOUS EXPERIENCE
   (A) *Teaching*

| Position | Name of School | Type | No. of Years |
|---|---|---|---|
| (i) | | | |
| (ii) | | | |
| (iii) | | | |

   (B) *Non Teaching*

| Position | Name of Employer | No. of Years | Any relevant comment |
|---|---|---|---|
| (i) | | | |
| (ii) | | | |
| (iii) | | | |

5  TRAINING

| Years | University/College | Qualifications | (If degree please state class) |
|---|---|---|---|
| (i) | | | |
| (ii) | | | |
| (iii) | | | |

6  ANY FURTHER QUALIFICATIONS, ETC.

# Part II

In this section we are interested in your attitudes to general questions of educational policy within the school. We hope that all staff will feel able to make some comment on these questions. If you wish to expand any answers please do so on the reverse side of the sheet.

7  Why did you come to this particular school?

8  Were you in favour of Comprehensive Education when you came?

9  Do you still feel the same or have you changed your views in any way?

10  What do you see as the purpose of education in this locality? Are there any special advantages or problems?

11  Does the *comprehensive* system of education have, in your opinion, a different function from other types (e.g. tripartite, private)? If so, what is it?

12  Does the co-educational nature of Ruffwood help or hinder your work as a teacher?

13  Have you any views about the amount of time which should be devoted to different subjects on the curriculum?

14  Or about the manner the subjects could be most advantageously presented? (either in general or in relationship to your own subject).

15  We would like to have some understanding of what you think the role of a teacher should be at this school. For instance, should the teacher try to inculcate middle class standards or should he accept the values of the surrounding locality? Please comment on this question with special

F

reference to matters such as slang, manners, ambition of the children, appearance of the children, etc.

16  Do you think that you should pass on your own religious views to the children?

17  Do you think that you should pass on your own political views to the children?

18  Turning to the organisation of the school, are there any ways in which you think it could be improved?

19  Do you prefer the horizontal (year groups, forms) or the vertical (houses, tutorial sets) method of organisation?

20  Does the size of the school hinder its effective working or does it allow for greater scope and variety of subjects? Please comment.

21  Do you think that most children have a reasonably close contact with at least one member of staff?

22  Is there any section of the pupils whose interests are being overlooked? (We include a 'prompt list' which is by no means exhaustive—please tick in the appropriate place and, if you wish, expand your answer).

|       |                                                        | Boys | Girls | Both |
|-------|--------------------------------------------------------|------|-------|------|
| (i)   | Academic                                               | Boys | Girls | Both |
| (ii)  | Moderate academic, e.g. '6 years to "O" level'         | Boys | Girls | Both |
| (iii) | Remedial or backward                                   | Boys | Girls | Both |
| (iv)  | 2nd quartile— future apprentices, nurses, secretaries, etc. | Boys | Girls | Both |
| (v)   | Those just above remedial classes (3rd quartile)       | Boys | Girls | Both |
| (vi)  | Maladjusted                                            | Boys | Girls | Both |
| (vii) | Delinquent                                             | Boys | Girls | Both |
| (viii)| 4th year leavers                                       | Boys | Girls | Both |

(ix) 1st year      2nd year      3rd year
     4th year      5th year      6th year
(x) Those in particular courses     If so, which
(xi) Other (please comment)

23 Should more or less attention be given to any of the following aspects of school life? (Please ring relevant answer.)

|  |  | More | Less | About right | Don't know | No Ans. |
|---|---|---|---|---|---|---|
| (i) | Practical subjects | M | L | AR | DN | NA |
| (ii) | Politics | M | L | AR | DN | NA |
| (iii) | Religious life and education | M | L | AR | DN | NA |
| (iv) | Social training | M | L | AR | DN | NA |
| (v) | Academic subjects | M | L | AR | DN | NA |
| (vi) | Outside activities— clubs | M | L | AR | DN | NA |
| (vii) | — 63 Society | M | L | AR | DN | NA |
| (viii) | — Ormside etc.— camping | M | L | AR | DN | NA |
| (ix) | Drama, Art, Cine-clubs | M | L | AR | DN | NA |
| (x) | Visual aids, e.g. films | M | L | AR | DN | NA |
| (xi) | P.E. and sport | M | L | AR | DN | NA |
| (xii) | English subjects | M | L | AR | DN | NA |
| (xiii) | History | M | L | AR | DN | NA |
| (xiv) | Geography | M | L | AR | DN | NA |
| (xv) | Science | M | L | AR | DN | NA |
| (xvi) | Technical subjects | M | L | AR | DN | NA |
| (xvii) | Vocations subjects | M | L | AR | DN | NA |
| (xviii) | Maths | M | L | AR | DN | NA |
| (xix) | Education on sex | M | L | AR | DN | NA |
| (xx) | Domestic subjects | M | L | AR | DN | NA |
| (xxi) | Music | M | L | AR | DN | NA |
| (xxii) | Art | M | L | AR | DN | NA |
| (xxiii) | Other please specify and comment | M | L | AR | DN | NA |

# Part III

In the following section we would like your comments on the following topics (some of which you may have covered in your answers to previous questions). Please do not feel compelled to comment on all topics which have been put forward as suggestions; on the other hand we hope you will raise any questions which we have inadvertently omitted and would value any answers which you are able to give.

Could you comment on: —

24 The hierarchy of the staff. Communications between senior and junior staff. Do you ever, for instance, learn facts from the children which you feel you should have learnt by another method?

25 On the age distribution of the staff.

26 On the relative roles of the houses and the academic departments.

27 The provision of teaching facilities and aids (e.g. books, projectors).

28 Communication between members of staff.

29 Could you estimate the number of teachers with whom you have had regular contact during the past term?

*No.*

(a) In connection with your duties as a teacher/tutor
(b) Socially

30 Are you satisfied/dissatisfied with the amount of contact with your colleagues?

31 Would you like to comment on the provision of organised social activities for the staff?

32 Is the Daily Bulletin an effective means of communication?

33 Are tutorial groups in your opinion effective?

34 Would you like to comment on house/school assemblies?

35 — On school discipline?

36 (a) Are you in favour of caning?
   (b) Do you (or if you were in a position to, would you) use it?

Would you like to comment on
37 House organisation.

38 Subject departments.

39 Homework

40 Provision of recreation, sports, etc.

41 Outside activities—clubs.

42 The provision of leisure activities for adolescents within Kirkby itself.

43 Do you find the children you teach responsive (or apathetic) to their work? Does this vary according to age and/or ability? Please specify.

44 Would you like to make any comparison between children in Ruffwood and others you may have taught?

45 Are the pupils at Ruffwood co-operative? Does this vary according to age or ability? Boys or girls? Is there any difference between attitudes inside and outside the classroom. Please comment.

46 What about the parents? Do you find them interested in the work of the school?

47 Could you comment on F.R.S.A.

48 FOR HEADMASTERS (OR HEADMISTRESSES) AND HOUSE-MASTERS ONLY

How many of the children's parents have you or your tutors seen during the last school year?

Both parents

Father only

Mother only

Would you like to comment (especially relating to frequency of contact and type of parent seen, e.g. parents of 'good', 'bad' or 'indifferent' pupils)?

49 FOR ALL STAFF

Is there, in your opinion, any connection between family background and attitudes and/or ability of the children you teach? Please specify.

50 Would you like to comment on delinquency in relationship to the training provided at Ruffwood?

51 Do you think there are marked social distinctions (e.g. respectable, non respectable) among the pupils?
If so, are these inspired by parental attitudes?

52 Do the children make any distinction amongst themselves on the basis of academic ability?

53 Are you aware of any racial barriers or do different 'colours' mix equally? Again, could you comment on the home influence (if any)?

54 Have you any opinion on the streaming/non-streaming controversy?

55 Would you like to comment on the opinion, best expressed in the Spens and Norwood reports, 'that some children should work with their hands and others with their brains'?

56 Do you agree to the proposals for re-organisation along comprehensive lines in areas where there are long established schools?

57 Are you in favour of school uniform? If so, why?

58 A particular problem appears to be the question of nylons and make-up for girls; would you like to make any suggestions about this topic?

59 Should staff be paid for outside activities or is this an integral part of their vocation?

60 What is your opinion about the present rates of pay for the teaching profession?

61 Would you also like to comment, either generally or in relation to Ruffwood, on the availability of posts of special responsibility (e.g. graded posts and Heads of Departments).

# Part IV

The following questions are directed primarily towards those who have a responsibility for the placing of children in their future occupations.

62 What opportunities or problems will face the following types of leaver in gaining jobs? Please comment on some or all, and do not be confined by the categories which we have suggested.
   (a) The academic boy
   (b) The academic girl

    (c) Boys in obtaining apprenticeships. Do you feel that the present method of selection and of training apprentices is satisfactory or unsatisfactory, bearing in mind the comparative novelty of such children taking the G.C.E. (or C.S.E.)?

    (d) The above average (yet non-academic) girl who will perhaps seek an opening in office-work or nursing

    (e) 3rd quartile boys (average and below)

    (f) 3rd quartile girls (average and below)

    (g) backward boys

    (h) Backward girls

63    Would you agree with Mr C. Boot, H.M. of the Christopher Wren (*Comprehensive*) School who wrote (p. 71, 'Inside the Comprehensive School', an N.U.T. publication) 'It is absolutely evident that, although some sixth formers will take the usual route to the university and its degrees, far more will proceed to technical college or training college at the end of the seventh year.' Is this, do you consider, the aim of Ruffwood?

64    Is there in Kirkby any danger of over-training (especially in relationship to apprenticeships; e.g. too many capable children for too few jobs), or on the contrary do you feel that there are far too few able children to fill the jobs at present available?

65    Does a similar situation (too many girls for too few jobs or vice versa) apply to able non-academic girls?

66    Are you happy or unhappy about the present employment situation which faces school leavers in Kirkby? Why?

67    Are there any special problems connected with the education and future careers for girls?

68    What role do you foresee for the Kirkby College of Further Education in relationship to the school?

69 Do you think that the school's connections with industry could be closer, and if so, in what way could they be improved?

70 Do you get all the cooperation from parents that you could wish in choosing courses/careers for pupils? Please comment fully.

71 Who should make the choice regarding a pupil's future course/career?
(*a*) School      (*b*) Parent      (*c*) Child
(*d*) Combination (please comment)

72 Would you like to say anything about the Youth Employment Service for the future of Ruffwood's children?

# *Part V*

If you would prefer not to reply to the following questions, please omit them and write 'Prefer not to reply' in the spaces provided.

73 We are interested as to how you view your prospects of advancement—or should we say of a future career—bearing in mind that you are teaching in this particular school. Would you like to make any remarks about this?

74 At what age did you decide to become a teacher?

75 Which qualification would you consider was most necessary for a teacher? (Please weight your answer on the basis of 5 points,
e.g. (*a*) 5 (*b*) 0 or (*a*) 1 (*b*) 4.

No. of points

(*a*) Ability to teach
(*b*) Knowledge of subject to be taught

_____

Total     5

_____

76 How long do you intend to remain in the school? (Please tick as appropriate.)
  (i) For a few years (1/2)          (iv) Don't know
  (ii) For a time (3/5)              (v) Prefer not to reply
  (iii) For a longer period (5 +)

77 Would you like to comment on your reasons for staying/ leaving (e.g. marriage, promotion, family, experience, etc.).

78 Finally, bearing in mind that the question of comprehensive education is a particularly vexed one at the moment, could you tell us for which political party you intend to vote in the next election. (Please tick.)

Conservative
Liberal
Labour
Communist
Other
None
Do not know
Prefer not to reply

We are certain that there will be many topics which we have not mentioned either because we were not aware of them or because they only apply to your own specific position (e.g. Deputy Head, Careers Master, Master i/c Ormside). We would be extremely grateful if you would raise these questions below and tell us what ideas you have about them. We hope that if there are any advantages or problems connected with the running of the school, or any general points that you would like to raise, that you will take the opportunity to do so here. Moreover, we would be particularly interested in comments on any questions which we feel we could investigate during the rest of this survey. May we sincerely thank you for your cooperation.

# *Appendix C*

*Ruffwood School: Pupils' Questionaire*

This is a survey conducted by the University of Liverpool. The answers you give will NOT be seen by anyone in the school and will be kept quite confidential. We are interested in your experiences at school and your plans for employment as well as in your leisure time activities. The answers you give will help us to advise the authorities in planning for the future and so will help other teenagers like yourself. Please give honest and sensible answers. Will you tick the appropriate answer, or if there are no alternatives, write in your answer in the spaces provided.

NAME                     BOY     GIRL

                                  (Please tick)

FORM OR GENERAL SET

HOUSE                    AGE    Years    Months

1   Do you intend staying on at school and going into the 5th form? (That means staying on after the law allows you to go to work.)
Yes     No     (Please tick)

2   Is this what you yourself want to do?
Yes     No     (Please tick)

3 Do your parents want you to stay on at school?
Yes        No        Don't mind        (Please tick)

4 If your answer to Question 1 was Yes—or No—can you tell us why?

5 If your answer to Question 1 was No, have your teachers suggested that it is not worth your while staying on an extra year?
Yes        No        (Please tick)
(Do not answer this if you answered Yes to Question 1.)

6 Do you think that staying on at school and taking examinations will help you to earn more or less by the time you are about 21?
About the same        More        Less        Don't know

7 What job do you wish to get when you leave? (If you don't know, write NOT CERTAIN.) (Please be as exact as possible.)

8 Do you want to become an apprentice or train for a job in some way after you leave school?
Yes        No        Don't know        (Please tick)

9 What job do your parents want you to get?

10 What job have your teachers suggested for you? (If none, write in *None*.)

11 If you have a particular kind of job in mind, do you think than an extra year in Ruffwood will help you to get it?
Yes        No

12 In choosing a job, who influences you most?
Your parents
Teachers
Friends
Make up your own mind        (Please tick)

13 Are any of your close friends keen to get the same kind of job as you?
Yes     No


14 Are your close friends thinking of staying on into the 5th form or leaving in the 4th?
Staying on in 5th
Leaving in 4th
Some staying some leaving
Don't know


15 Do your friends ever come into your home?
Yes     No


16 Do you ever visit your friends' homes?
Yes     No


17 Do your parents disapprove of any of your friends?
Yes     No     They don't know them


18 Do you attend a church, chapel, lodge or Sunday School regularly? (say once a month or more).
Yes     No


19 If your answer to Question 18 is Yes, who do you go with? (for example: parents, friend (boy or girl), etc.).


20 How often do you go to a cinema?
Never or rarely
Less than once a week
Once a week
More than once a week          (Please tick)


21 How often do you go dancing?
Never or rarely
Less than once a week
Once a week
More than once a week

22  How often do you go to the Cavern or similar club?
    Never or rarely
    Less than once a week
    Once a week
    More than once a week

23  How often do you go to the school (youth) club?
    Never or rarely
    Once a week
    Occasionally

24  How often do you go to any other youth club (not
    counting the school club)?
    Never or rarely
    Less than once a week
    Once a week
    More than once a week

25  Have you any suggestions for improving Youth Clubs in
    Kirkby?

26  Who do you spend most of your leisure time with? (For
    example, friend (boy or girl), group of friends, etc.

27  Do you watch TV?
    A lot
    Some of the time
    Very little
    Never

28  Do you go to the Kirkby Public Library?
    Yes        No

29  What books, papers or magazines have you read out of
    school time during the last month? Please write down a
    few.

30  On average, how long does your homework take you? (Be honest, nobody will know.)

Do not do any
Less than $\frac{1}{4}$ hour
Between $\frac{1}{4}$ and $\frac{1}{2}$ hour
Between $\frac{1}{2}$ and 1 hour
Over 1 hour

31  How often do you go to Liverpool? (Please tick the nearest.)

Never
About once a month
About once a fortnight
About once a week
About twice a week
About three times a week
Four or more times a week

32  If you do go to Liverpool, please tick any of the following things you do. (You may tick more than one.)

Visit relatives
Mess about
Shopping
Pictures
Football Match
Dancing
Club
Other things (please write in)

33  FOR BOYS

Have you got a steady girl friend?
Yes      No

FOR GIRLS

Have you got a steady boy friend?
Yes      No

34 If your answer to Question 33 is Yes, what age is he or she?
Older than me
About the same age
Younger than me

35 There has been a lot of talk in Kirkby about gangs breaking up shop windows, throwing things on to railway lines, or beating people up. What do you think about these gangs?

36 If you saw someone breaking into Ruffwood School late at night, would you report it to the Police?
Yes        No

37 Which of the following teachers would you say you know best?
House Master
House Tutor
English Teacher
Any other (please write in)

38 Which of these members of staff would you go to if you had a problem?
House Master
House Tutor
English Teacher
Other Teacher (please write in)
None

39 When you are over 21, do you think you will want to go on living in Kirkby or do you hope to be able to move elsewhere?
Live in Kirkby        Move out        Don't mind

40 What new things would you like to see built in Kirkby?

# *Appendix D*

*Ruffwood School: Parents' Questionnaire*

NAME

ADDRESS

NAME OF OFFSPRING IN 3rd YEAR

*Circumstances of interview*
We are interested in education in Kirkby and wondered if you
would help us by answering a few questions.

1   What do you think about education at Ruffwood?
    Are you

| | *Wife's Response* | *Husband's Response* |
|---|---|---|
| Satisfied | | |
| Dissatisfied | | |
| No opinion | | |

2   What about Youth Clubs? What is your attitude to them?
    Should there be

| | *Wife's Response* | *Husband's Response* |
|---|---|---|
| More | | |
| Right number now | | |
| Would not be properly used by teenagers | | |

(Note any comment)

3 Do you think there is enough for young people to do in Kirkby?

| | Wife's Response | Husband's Response |
|---|---|---|
| Yes | | |
| No | | |
| About right | | |
| Don't know | | |

4 (If informants answer No to question 3, ask): —What would you like to see?
In particular, we are interested in boys and girls who may be leaving school in the near future. We believe that you have a son/daughter N who is about 14 at Ruffwood.
(If not—you are interviewing the wrong person!)

5 Is          staying on into the 5th form, e.g. after the legal leaving age, until he/she is 16? (If parents' responses differ, please note.)
Yes               No               Not certain

6 Did          want to stay or leave? (again note any differing response).
Stay               Leave               Not certain

7 Did you want          to stay or leave?

| | Wife's Response | Husband's Response |
|---|---|---|
| Preferred him/ her to stay | | |
| Preferred him/ her to leave | | |
| Not certain/ No definite opinion | | |

(Note any comments)

8 What did his/her teachers suggest?
Stay               Leave               Don't know
(Note differing response)

9 Can you tell us how many children you have? (including the child in the 3rd year at Ruffwood). How many boys and girls?

No. of boys                    No. of girls

10 Do you think schooling matters as much for girls as for boys?

|  | Wife's Response | Husband's Response |
|---|---|---|
| Same for girls | ———————— | ———————— |
| Less for girls | ———————— | ———————— |
| Don't know | ———————— | ———————— |

11 Can you tell me how often you have visited Ruffwood since July last (1964)?

|  | No. of Times |
|---|---|
| Answer for Wife | ———————— |
| Answer for Husband | ———————— |

12 Did you go to the meeting to discuss        's career? Or have you gone to the school to discuss with anyone concerning either whether        should stay on an extra year or regarding a job for him/her?

Both parents have been
Wife has been
Husband has been
Neither has been
Other (please specify)

13 If you did go—who did you meet?
Name of teacher (if known)                Status

14 Do you think teachers should use the cane?

|  | Wife's Response | Husband's Response |
|---|---|---|
| Yes, for boys | ———————— | ———————— |
| Yes for both boys and girls | ———————— | ———————— |
| No | ———————— | ———————— |
| Don't know/ not certain | ———————— | ———————— |

15 What job does          want to do?

16 Is this what you want him/her to do?

|  | Wife's Response | Husband's Response |
|---|---|---|
| Yes | | |
| No | | |
| Not certain | | |
| (Note comments) | | |

17 (If Question 16 is answered in negative, or if parents are doubtful, ask: What would you want him/her to do?)

18 What do you feel about          being apprenticed (*for boys*) or having more training after leaving school?

|  | Wife's Response | Husband's Response |
|---|---|---|
| In favour of apprenticeship/ training | | |
| Against | | |
| Neutral | | |

(Note responses in as much detail as possible)

19 What job do his/her teachers think          should do?

20 Do you think that an *extra* year of schooling will help or hinder          in getting or doing a job?

|  | Wife's Response | Husband's Response |
|---|---|---|
| Help | | |
| Hinder | | |
| Make little difference | | |
| Don't know | | |

(Note comments)

21 Do you agree with the raising of the school leaving age so that it will be compulsory to stay on at school until 16 years of age, in 1970?

|  | Wife's Response | Husband's Response |
|---|---|---|

| Agree | | |
|---|---|---|
| Disagree | | |
| Don't mind | | |
| Don't know | | |

22 Are you in favour of comprehensive, as opposed to grammar/secondary modern type of education?

|  | *Wife's Response* | *Husband's Response* |
|---|---|---|
| In favour of comprehensive | | |
| In favour of grammar secondary/ modern | | |
| Don't know | | |

23 If you had your time over again, would you stay on for extra schooling at a school like Ruffwood?

|  | *Wife's Response* | *Husband's Response* |
|---|---|---|
| Yes | | |
| No | | |
| Not certain | | |

24 (Engage in conversation re parents' education and ask what type of education and at what age they left school)

| Elementary only | | |
|---|---|---|
| Selective | | |
| Age on leaving | | |

25 Are you in favour or against school uniform?

|  | *Wife's Response* | *Husband's Response* |
|---|---|---|
| In favour | | |
| Against | | |
| In favour but for cost | | |
| Neutral/ No opinion | | |

26  Ruffwood School gives instruction to children about sex.
    Are you in favour of this or against it?

|            | Wife's Response | Husband's Response |
|------------|-----------------|--------------------|
| In favour  | ——————————————— | ———————————————— |
| Against    | ——————————————— | ———————————————— |
| Don't know | ——————————————— | ———————————————— |

27  Are you in favour or against          doing homework?

|            | Wife's Response | Husband's Response |
|------------|-----------------|--------------------|
| In favour  | ——————————————— | ———————————————— |
| Against    | ——————————————— | ———————————————— |
| Don't know | ——————————————— | ———————————————— |

28  Do you try to make          do it, or leave it to him/her?
    Try to get          to do it
    Leave it to
    (Note, if differing parental responses)

29  Where does he/she do it?
    Room by self
    Room with T.V.
    Shared room without T.V.
    Other
    (Please write in full comments)

30  Does          like to read serious books?
    Yes          No

31  What do you enjoy reading?

32  We are interested in problems of disciplining adolescents
    today. Have you any views on this?

33  Do you in any way exercise control over whom your
    children mix with, or do you leave it to them to pick their
    own friends.
    (Note any differing responses and comments)
    Exercise some control
    Leave it to them

34 There has been a lot of publicity in the Press about gangs and vandalism both in Kirkby and elsewhere. What do you think about this? Should anything be done?

Finally, a few questions about yourself—

35 (a) Husband's Occupation
   (b) Usual occupation (if different)

36 Wife's Occupation (if any)                Full / Part time
   Hours of work for mother
   (Detailed information re occupation should be obtained, e.g. whether apprenticed or not—engineer is not sufficient. Obtain information as to type of job, seniority, firm, etc.)

37 When did you move to Kirkby?              Year

38 Where did you move from?
   Street and District

39 What type of accommodation were you living in?
   (As detailed information as possible, e.g. whether flat, house, whether shared or not, type of house—terraced, semi-detached, etc., whether council property, private rent, owner-occupier, etc.)

40 Can you tell us why you moved?

41 Did you want to come to Kirkby? (Note comments)
   Yes          No          Did not mind

42 How do you like Kirkby now? (Note comments)
   Good          O.K.          Poor

43 How often do you visit Liverpool per week, other than for your job?

|  | *Wife's response* | *Husband's response* |
|---|---|---|
| No. of times | | |

44  What reasons do you go for? (other than occupation).
    (Tick all appropriate and write in any other reasons and
    comments)

|  | *Wife's response* | *Husband's response* |
|---|---|---|
| Visit relatives | ———————— | ———————— |
| Visit friends | ———————— | ———————— |
| Shopping | ———————— | ———————— |
| Pictures | ———————— | ———————— |
| Football |  |  |
| Match | ———————— | ———————— |
| Pub | ———————— | ———————— |
| Other (please write in) | ———————— | ———————— |

45  Finally, do you want your children to stay in Kirkby or
    leave it when they grow up? (Note comments)

|  | *Wife's response* | *Husband's response* |
|---|---|---|
| Stay | ———————— |  |
| Leave | ———————— |  |
| Don't mind, it's up to them | ———————— |  |

Thank you very much for helping us. Are there any
comments that you would like to make?

# Appendix E

## An Ormside Experiment

A WEEK IN SEPTEMBER WITH FOURTH YEAR LEAVERS

Eight o'clock in High Cup Gill. It's dark, the boys have finished their supper and washed up. Now is the time for all sensible campers to curl up in a sleeping-bag and go to sleep because there is nothing to stay up for and I've forgotten the candles. But peace doesn't come so easily with IV.J boys around.

Ominous noises come from the surrounding tents; there'll be a fight in five minutes. I must do something, I must exhaust these boys to prevent the tents being wrecked. Hastily a toilet-roll is stuck torch-like on a rock 200 yards away, defenders are chosen and attackers briefed to snatch just one sheet of paper without capture, a crazy game played over steep grass slopes and rocky streams, in the dark. When all variations on this theme are exhausted and interest flags, we turn to Hare and Hounds, the hare to blow his whistle every minute till caught. By 10 o'clock the party has squeezed into the teachers' tent for coffee and retired peacefully to bed.

It was a hectic week, deliberately. We hoped to cram into three and a half days as many varied, exciting and challenging activities as we could dream up, and we intended to feed the boys magnificently. The food was good, the boys said so freely; on the other hand it is easy to impress boys with simple food, well-cooked in reasonable quantity, when they confess to being fed on an inadequate diet at home. The activities were new to most of the lads with us; if not enjoyed at the time they provided an opportunity for hilarious reminiscence afterwards.

The programme included an introductory walk up Cross Fell on the Monday afternoon, thorough instruction in camp-cooking and tent erection on Tuesday morning, followed by a tiring walk into High Cup Gill for a night's camping. (The camp site in the Gill is superb, a deep cut valley, an impressive fringe of crags, a delightful beck, no sign of human habitation, an admirable space for energetic rampaging and, finally, ideal turf for pitching tents and sleeping on.) On Wednesday, a really fine day, we spent some time on the crags in High Cup Nick teaching the boys how to 'abseil', a spectacular but very safe technique of sliding down a cliff-face with a doubled rope. After a swim in the Gill we returned to Ormside for another swim in the Eden and supper. Thursday brought the Treasure Hunt a 10-mile expedition in pairs through the marvellous countryside around Ormside; this involves accurate following of route instructions, the collection of country-type items and the answering of about 50 questions en route.

To ensure that the lads got their money's worth we fixed up an Arnhem Trail after the Treasure Hunt, 200 yards of string threaded through bushes, up a tree, into a ditch, down a steep hill and finally through a chest-deep stream twice. This string has to be followed blindfold!

To sum up, the boys appeared to enjoy themselves immensely, not only because it was an escape from school. For the teachers it was also enjoyable, rewarding and extremely hard work.

# *Appendix F*

## *Additional Tables*

TABLE 6.1. COMPARISON BETWEEN CERTAIN CHARACTERISTICS OF
KIRKBY AND NON-KIRKBY SURVEY RESIDENTS AND THEIR CHILDREN

|  | *Non-Kirkby Residents:* No. | *Kirkby Residents:* No. |
|---|---|---|
| Sex: Male | 7 | 112 |
| Female | 8 | 90 |
| **Social Class of Parent:** | | |
| Social Class I | 1 | — |
| Social Class II | 3 | 5 |
| Social Class III, non-manual | 1 | 15 |
| Social Class III, manual | 7 | 92 |
| Social Class IV, non-manual | — | 2 |
| Social Class IV, manual | 3 | 52 |
| Social Class V | — | 19 |
| None, retired, etc. | — | 17 |
| **School Set:** | | |
| 1 | 2 | 29 |
| 2 | 11 | 24 |
| 3 | 2 | 53 |
| 4 | — | 84 |
| 5 | — | 12 |
| **Social Class of Child's Chosen Occupation:** | | |
| Social Class I | — | 7 |
| Social Class II | 6 | 24 |
| Social Class III, non-manual | 4 | 39 |
| Social Class III, manual | 2 | 65 |
| Social Class IV, non-manual | 1 | 4 |
| Social Class IV, manual | 1 | 11 |
| Social Class V | — | 6 |
| Other, no answer | 1 | 46 |
| Wish to stay for additional year | 14 | 111 |
| Do not wish to stay for additional year | 1 | 88 |
| Don't know | — | 3 |

TABLE 6.2. SOCIAL CLASS OF OCCUPATION CHOSEN BY PUPILS AT RUFFWOOD, EALING AND N.W. LANCS SCHOOLS

| Social Class of Occupation | Ruffwood | | | | Ealing Sec. Modern Schools[1] 1948* | | N. W. Lancs. Sec. Modern Schools[2] 1949–50* | |
|---|---|---|---|---|---|---|---|---|
| | Boys | | Girls | | Boys | Girls | Boys | Girls |
| | No. | % | No. | % | % of 824 | % of 801 | % of 56 | % of 77 |
| 1 | 6 | 5 | 1 | } 18 | – | – } | 6 | – |
| 2 | 13 | 11 | 17 | | 4 | 3 } | | 2 |
| 3 { N.M. | 5 | 4 | 38 | 39 | } 58 | } 72 | | – |
| 3 { M. | 61 | 51 | 6 | 6 | | | } 51 | 60 |
| 4 { N.M | – | – | 5 | 8 | } 32 | } 20 | | – |
| 4 { M. | 4 | 3 | 8 | 8 | | | } 43 | } 38 |
| 5 | 1 | } 3 | 5 | 5 | 6 | 5 | – | – |
| Forces (unspec) | 2 | | – | – | – | – | – | – |
| None given | 27 | 23 | 18 | 19 | – | – | – | – |
| Total | 119 | 100 | 98 | 100 | 100 | 100 | 100 | 100 |

* Hall-Jones scale.                N.M.  Non-manual
[1] From M. Wilson, op. cit.        M.    Manual
[2] From G. Jahoda, op. cit.

TABLE 6.3. SOCIAL CLASS OF PARENT COMPARED WITH THAT OF PUPIL'S CHOSEN OCCUPATION

| Social Class of Parent. | 1 | 2 | 3 N.M. | 3 M. | 4 N.M. | 4 M. | 5 | Forces unspec. | No. answer | Total No. | % |
|---|---|---|---|---|---|---|---|---|---|---|---|
| 1 | | | | 1 | | | | | | 1 | ⎫ 4 |
| 2 | 1 | 1 | 3 | 2 | | 1 | | | | 8 | ⎬ |
| 3 { N.M. | – | 5 | 5 | 3 | | | 1 | | 2 | 16 | 7 |
| 3 { M. | 5 | 17 | 18 | 28 | 3 | 4 | 2 | | 22 | 99 | 46 |
| 4 { N.M. | | | | 1 | | | | 1 | 2 | 2 | 1 |
| 4 { M. | | 6 | 12 | 21 | 2 | 3 | | | 11 | 55 | 25 |
| 5 | | | 3 | 7 | | 3 | 2 | | 4 | 19 | 9 |
| None, retired, no answer etc. | 1 | 1 | 2 | 4 | | 1 | 1 | 1 | 6 | 17 | 8 |
| Total No, | 7 | 30 | 43 | 67 | 5 | 12 | 6 | 2 | 45 | 217 | – |
| % | 3 | 14 | 20 | 31 | 2 | 5 | 3 | 1 | 21 | – | 100 |

N.M. Non-manual
M. Manual

TABLE 6.4. PUPILS SET AND CHOSEN OCCUPATION

| Set | 1 | 2 | 3 N.M. | 3 M. | 4 N.M. | 4 M. | 5 | Forces unspec. | No answer | Total |
|---|---|---|---|---|---|---|---|---|---|---|
| 1 | 6 | 12 | 5 | 4 | | | | | 4 | 31 |
| 2 | | 9 | 9 | 9 | 1 | 1 | 1 | | 5 | 35 |
| 3 | | 6 | 18 | 19 | | 3 | | 1 | 8 | 55 |
| 4 | 1 | 3 | 11 | 30 | 3 | 8 | 4 | 1 | 23 | 84 |
| 5 | | | | 5 | 1 | | 1 | | 5 | 12 |
| Total | 7 | 30 | 43 | 67 | 5 | 12 | 6 | 2 | 45 | 217 |

N.M. Non-manual
M. Manual

TABLE 6.5. PUPILS' AND PARENTS' ATTITUDE TO KIRKBY

| When over 21 years | Parents by Social Class | | | | | | | | Total | | | | Pupils | |
| | S.C. 1&2 | | S.C. 3 | | S.C. 4 & 5 | | No occupation Retired etc. | | | | | | | |
| | Husband | Wife | Husband | Wife | Husband | Wife | Husband | Wife | Husband No. | % | Wife No. | % | No. | % |
| Wish (them) to stay in Kirkby | — | 1 | 17 | 16 | 12 | 18 | — | 2 | 29 | 13 | 37 | 17 | 34 | 16 |
| Wish (them) to leave Kirkby | 1 | 2 | 21 | 22 | 8 | 11 | 3 | 6 | 33 | 15 | 41 | 19 | 96 | 44 |
| Don't mind / Don't know | 4 | 3 | 51 | 66 | 43 | 38 | 8 | 12 | 106 | 49 | 119 | 55 | 66 | 30 |
| Not applicable / No answer / Not present | 4 | 3 | 26 | 11 | 8 | 4 | 11 | 2 | 49 | 23 | 20 | 9 | 21 | 10 |
| Total | 9 | 9 | 115 | 115 | 71 | 71 | 22 | 22 | 217 | 100 | 217 | 100 | 217 | 100 |

TABLE 6.7. PARENTS' ATTITUDE TO SEX INSTRUCTION

| Attitude to Sex Instruction | Husband | | Wife | |
|---|---|---|---|---|
| | Number | Per cent | Number | Per cent |
| In favour | 165 | 90 | 177 | 83 |
| Against | 12 | 7 | 25 | 12 |
| Don't know | 6 | 3 | 11 | 5 |
| Not present at interview | 34 | Excluded | 4 | Excluded |
| Total | 217 | 100 | 217 | 100 |

TABLE 8.6. KIRKBY AMENITIES SUGGESTED BY PUPILS AND PARENTS (KIRKBY RESIDENTS ONLY)

| | Pupils | | Parents | |
|---|---|---|---|---|
| | Number | Per cent of amenities suggested | Number | Per cent of amenities suggested |
| Swimming baths | 156 | 27 | 93 | 20 |
| Cinema | 150 | 25 | 118 | 27 |
| Sport facilities | 98 | 17 | 93 | 20 |
| Youth clubs and organisations | 52 | 9 | 42 | 9 |
| Dance Hall | 31 | 5 | 65 | 14 |
| Shops, houses, flats, etc. | 43 | 7 | — | — |
| Parks, amusements, etc. | 32 | 5 | — | — |
| Theatre, museum, zoo. | 6 | 1 | — | — |
| Educational facilities | 5 | 1 | 9 | 2 |
| Community Hall | — | — | 5 | 1 |
| Bingo, gambling | — | — | 2 | — |
| Don't know, No response | 8 | 1 | 5 | 1 |
| Other | 10 | 2 | 28 | 6 |
| Total | 591 | 100 | 460 | 100 |